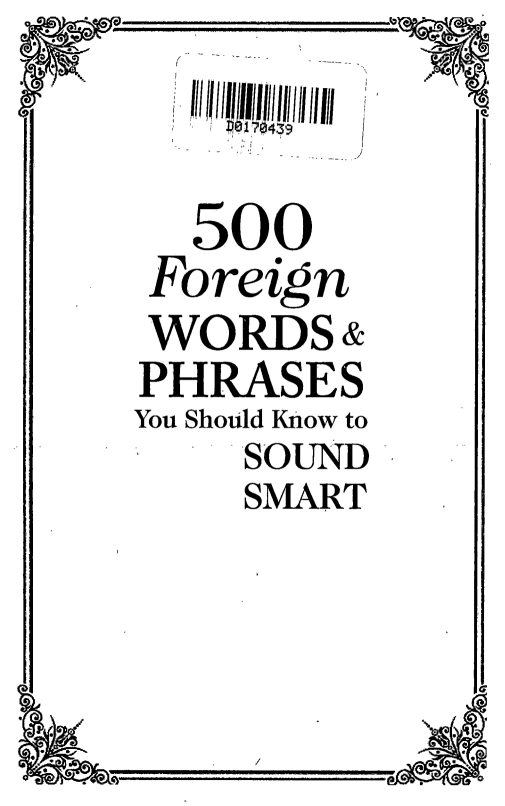

500
Foreign
WORDS &
PHRASES
You Should Know to
SOUND
SMART

500
Foreign
WORDS &
PHRASES
You Should Know to

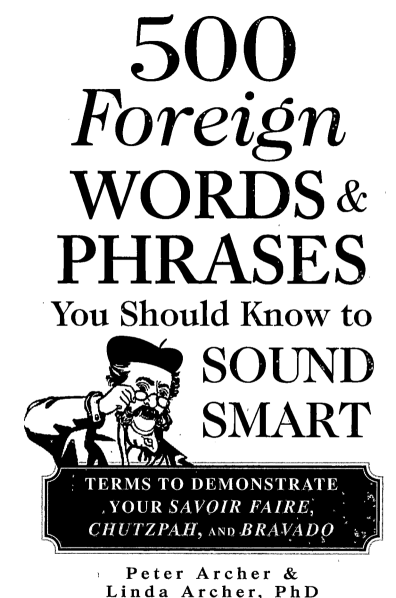

SOUND
SMART

TERMS TO DEMONSTRATE YOUR *SAVOIR FAIRE*, *CHUTZPAH*, AND *BRAVADO*

Peter Archer &
Linda Archer, PhD

Adamsmedia
Avon, Massachusetts

Published by
Adams Media, a division of F+W Media, Inc.
57 Littlefield Street, Avon, MA 02322. U.S.A.
www.adamsmedia.com

ISBN 10: 1-4405-4075-6
ISBN 13: 978-1-4405-4075-2
eISBN 10: 1-4405-4107-8
eISBN 13: 978-1-4405-4107-0

Printed in the United States of America.

10 9 8 7 6 5 4

Library of Congress Cataloging-in-Publication Data
is available from the publisher.

This publication is designed to provide accurate and authoritative information with regard to the subject matter covered. It is sold with the understanding that the publisher is not engaged in rendering legal, accounting, or other professional advice. If legal advice or other expert assistance is required, the services of a competent professional person should be sought.

—From a *Declaration of Principles* jointly adopted by a Committee of the American Bar Association and a Committee of Publishers and Associations

This book is available at quantity discounts for bulk purchases.
For information, please call 1-800-289-0963.

Contents

Dedication

For Jocelyn and Tim
Amor vincit omnia.

Acknowledgments

Thanks to Meredith O'Hayre and Katie Corcoran Lytle for their considerable support and assistance and to all the other great people at Adams Media. Especially, thanks to Karen Cooper for inviting us to write this book.

Introduction

When, in 1883, Emma Lazarus penned her sonnet "The New Colossus," she perhaps did not anticipate what a can of worms she was opening up.

Give me your tired, your poor,
Your huddled masses yearning to breathe free,
The wretched refuse of your teeming shore.

And they came. In the last decades of the nineteenth century and the opening years of the twentieth, millions arrived in America, having made the long journey from Europe in search of a brighter future. They brought with them the clothes on their backs and little else—save their languages. From Hester Street in Manhattan to the Haymarket in Chicago, a *patois* of foreign words and phrases filled the air.

The result, not surprisingly, was that American English grew infinitely richer, a stew of foreign words and phrases tossed together and poured out over the land. While most of the immigrants in time learned the language of their adopted country, their linguistic legacy remained.

Early English Roots

English, of course, has always borrowed from other tongues. Britain, in the first century A.D., became a province of the Roman Empire, and thus the upper classes—as well as many common people—were fluent in Latin. When the Romans retreated in the fourth century to deal unsuccessfully with the barbarian hordes threatening the Eternal City, they were replaced by invading Germanic tribes—the Angles, the Saxons, the Jutes, and others. Thus over the following centuries the remnants of Latin merged with Germanic/Scandinavian languages, often carried across the North Sea on the dragon prows of Viking longboats. From this emerged Anglo-Saxon, the language of *Beowulf* and the early kings of Britain.

It might have remained so if William of Normandy hadn't beaten the snot out of Harold Godwinson at the Battle of Hastings in 1066. The invading Normans were French-speaking (that is, they spoke an early form of French), and since they were now the ruling class of England, Norman French became the tongue of the upper classes. By the time Geoffrey Chaucer wrote *The Canterbury Tales* in the late fourteenth century, English had become more or less recognizable as something related to what we speak today.

Still, the slew of foreign words remained. Because English (and later American) law relied heavily on Roman legal concepts, many Latin legal terms were and are still used (although you could probably throw a lot of bricks in the region of a courthouse and not endanger any lawyers capable of speaking Latin).

Italian terms spread, partly as a result of the popularity of Italian cuisine, both in England and in America. The same thing happened to French cooking terms, particularly after the publication of *Mastering the Art of French Cooking* by Julia Child in 1961. (Before then, most Americans wouldn't have known a sauté pan from a stock pot if you'd belted them over the head with it.)

Spanish words came into common usage after the American conquest of the Southwest in the nineteenth century and in the twentieth century after the growth of the Hispanic population in all parts of the country. In the twentieth century, particularly during the counter-cultural decade of the 1960s, Sanskrit terms such as *dharma* became popular among young people discovering the mystic traditions of the East—or, at any rate, what they interpreted as the mystic traditions.

The Joys of Foreign Words

The charm of all these words and phrases is partly that they serve to remind us of our complex linguistic heritage, something too few people today take the time to think about. Amid the spread of the ghastly phenomenon known as "Textish," it does us good to contemplate the long, tortuous journey of our Mother Tongue.

There's an added benefit in knowing the sorts of words and phrases that are listed in this book: Using them can make you seem smart.

That's a bit curious, when you think about it. There's no evidence that the Romans of 2,000 years ago, for instance, were any more intelligent than we are. After all, their empire was brought down and divided up by people called Goths and Vandals. But despite that epic collapse, toss out a quotation or two in Latin at a cocktail party and you'll find people hanging on your every word. (On the other hand, how many people today speak Goth or Vandal? Not too damn many, that's for sure!)

Seasoning your conversation with *bon mots*, whether in French or Italian, can make you sound sophisticated and cool. People will imagine you sauntering down the Champs Élysées, stopping to sip a glass of wine at a sidewalk café and sample a succulent cheese or pastry. They'll see you lounging in a trattoria on a street off the Piazza San Marco in Venice, your espresso in front of you, as you exchange cheerful banter with the gondoliers.

Closer to home, they'll see you as the kind of person who gets invited to parties at the offices of the *New Yorker* or *Vanity Fair*, when you can rub elbows with the cognoscenti and exchange witticisms with writers and editors wearing tweed jackets with patches on the elbows, smelling of pipe tobacco and literature.

In fact, after reading this book, you might want to get such a jacket.

For each word in this book, we've included a pronunciation guide (since nothing says *poseur* like mispronouncing a foreign phrase) as well as background information on who said some of these things and why. That way you can doubly impress people when you remark, "As Julius Caesar said in 43 B.C. when crossing the Rubicon, '*Alea iacta est.*'" We've also included sample sentences to show how these words and phrases might be injected into ordinary conversation.

The downside of using a word or term from a foreign language is that your listeners may think you actually speak it. If you observe to a casual companion, "*Je ne regrette rien,*" you may be taken aback if he suddenly bursts into a flood of French that leaves you standing dazed and confused. The solution to such a circumstance is to cough quickly into your drink, pretend to choke, and murmur, "'*Scusez-moi*" as you hastily seek friendlier fields for conversation.

Above all, we hope this book implants in you an appreciation of the beauty of language and the multitude of purposes to which it can be put. And if it helps you impress your friends and acquaintances and get dates—well, that's cool too.

—*Wareham, Massachusetts, December 2011*

"Those who know nothing of foreign languages know nothing of their own."

—*Johann Wolfgang von Goethe*

ab aeterno (Latin) (ab eye-TER-no) (adv.)
Since the beginning of time.

> *AB AETERNO, men have wondered why precisely women need all those shoes. And women have wondered why men never listen and never ask directions.*

ab extra (Latin) (ab EX-tra) (adv.)
From without, or from an outside source.

> *Most political campaigns are funded by AB EXTRA contributions, although they prefer to paint themselves otherwise.*

ab imo pectore (Latin) (ab EE-mo pek-TO-ray) (adv.)
From the bottom of my heart; literally, "From the deepest part of my chest."

> *I love you madly, deeply, AB IMO PECTORE.*

ab initio (Latin) (ab in-IT-eeo) (adv.)
From the beginning; from the origin.

> *AB INITIO, the universe has been subject to the inviolable laws of gravity—something many college students discover both in the classroom and on Friday nights when leaving the campus bar.*

ab origine (Latin) (ab or-I-gin-ay) (adv.)
From the origin or beginning. Note that the term *abort* is literally to "un-arise," while the term *aborigine* is derived from the original meaning of the phrase, meaning people who were there in the beginning.

> *Native Americans were inhabitants of the North American continent AB ORIGINE, whereas Caucasians arrived only beginning in 1492.*

absente reo (Latin) (ab-SENT-ay RAY-oh) (adv.)
A legal term, meaning in the absence of the defendant.

> *Your Honor, ABSENTE REO, I would like to move for a mistrial, on the grounds that a defendant must be present when he is being prosecuted.*

absit iniuri verbis (Latin) (AB-sit in-YUR-ee WER-bis) (phrase)
Let injury through words not occur. More colloquially, Don't take offense at what I'm saying.

ABSIT INIURI VERBIS, you're a disgusting excuse for a human being who should choke on his own vomit. But I hope you won't take that the wrong way.

Nota Bene

Although you might think that it's illegal to say hurtful things about someone that aren't true, in fact the slander laws in the United States are remarkable for their elasticity. After a 1964 court case, *New York Times Co. v. Sullivan*, public figures who sued for slander or defamation had to prove that whoever published the information knew it was false but went ahead and published it anyway. This has meant that comparatively few libel suits in the United States are successful.

A

absit omen (Latin) (AB-sit OH-men) (phrase)
May the omen not occur. An expression of good will, since omens were taken extremely seriously by the Romans. Recall that Julius Caesar was warned by a soothsayer to beware the Ides of March. And look what happened to him when he ignored the advice.
I've got a very bad feeling about how things may turn out for you next week, ABSIT OMEN.

ab uno disce omnes (Latin) (ab OO-no DIS-kay AHM-nayz) (phrase)
From one, learn to know all. From Virgil's (70 B.C.–19 B.C.) *The Aeneid*, this references a circumstance in which one example can be taken to show an overriding principle.
Most cats spend most of their days and nights sleeping or eating; AB UNO DISCE OMNES we may reasonably deduce that cats are superior to humans.

ab urbe condita (Latin) (ab OOR-bay KON-dee-tah) (phrase)
From the founding of the city. Refers particularly to Rome, which, according to legend, was founded in 753 B.C. by the brothers Romulus and Remus. Abbreviated A.U.C., this was used as one of several dating systems until the early Middle Ages in Europe.
The Battle of Poitiers took place in 1488 AB URBE CONDITA and determined the course of European history.

> **Nota Bene**
> Early historians used a variety of systems for dating, including
> *ab urbe condita* (from the founding of the city [of Rome]) as
> well as dating from the crucifixion of Jesus, the creation of the
> world, and other events. In the sixth century, an Eastern monk,
> Dionysius Exiguus (c. 470–c. 544), developed a system of dat-
> ing based on the supposed incarnation of Christ. This system
> gained little acceptance during his lifetime, but in the eighth
> century the Venerable Bede (c. 673–735) used it in his seminal
> work *Historia Ecclesiastica Gentis Anglorum.* The popularity
> of this book ensured that this would become the standard dat-
> ing system all over Western Europe and from there, the world.
> Hence we date events either B.C. (Before Christ) or A.D. (Anno
> Domini). In recent years, these systems have been changed to
> B.C.E (Before Common Era) and C.E. (Common Era).

Abyssus abyssum invocat (Latin) (a-BISS-us a-BISS-oom in-WO-kat) (phrase)
Deep calls to deep. From Psalm 42. The usual interpretation is
that the singer is calling out to God, from whom he feels distant.
Another possible interpretation is that someone or something pro-
found finds an echo in something else meaningful.
> *You've moved me very deeply, and I feel I've found a kindred spirit
> in you. ABYSSUS ABYSSUM INVOCAT.*

a capella (Latin) (ah kap-PEH-lah) (adj.)
In the manner of the church or in the manner of the chapel. This is
applied to singing without accompaniment. Among those in recent
musical traditions who have attempted a capella singing are Bobby
McFerrin and the Manhattan Transfer.
> *Sweet Honey in the Rock is a well-known A CAPELLA group with
> an ability to mix a complex variety of harmonies.*

ad absurdum (Latin) (ad ab-SIR-dum) (adv.)
Literally, "reduction to absurdity." In argument, this is a way of dis-
proving a proposition by following it out to its logical, and absurd,
conclusion.

If we follow your argument that lowering tax rates always raises income, then logically, AD ABSURDUM, lowering the rate to 0 percent would result in infinite revenues.

ad arbitrium (Latin) (ad ar-BIT-ree-um) (adv.)
Arbitrarily. At will. Usually used in legal circles, but you can impress friends by tossing this into random conversations.

I find it silly that fashions change AD ARBITRIUM; when Seventh Avenue says "Change," we all change, rather than telling Versace to go to Hell.

Ad astra per alia porci (Latin) (ad AS-tra AH-lee-ah POR-kee) (phrase)
Although the phrase *ad astra,* meaning "to the stars," originated from the Latin poet Virgil (70 B.C.–19 B.C.), the American writer John Steinbeck (1902–1968) adopted as his symbol a winged pig (called Pigasus) and the motto *Ad astra per alia porci* (To the stars on the wings of a pig). Interestingly, in 1968 during the demonstrations accompanying the Democratic National Convention in Chicago, the Yippies (Youth International Party) led by Abbie Hoffman and Jerry Rubin, nominated a pig named Pigasus for president.

ad astra per aspera (Latin) (ad AS-truh per ASS-per-uh) (phrase)
To the stars, through hope. This has been adopted as the motto of many institutions, including the Milwaukee High School of the Arts, the Trenton Air Cadet Summer Training Centre in Canada, and Starfleet Academy.

addendum (Latin) (ah-DEN-doom) (noun)
An addition to a document after its printing. The Latin literally means, "something that must be added."
My latest book, which ran to 750 pages, now includes an essential ADDENDUM that further proves my whole argument.

ad fontes (Latin) (ad FON-tez) (adv.)
To the sources. It was particularly applied to the efforts of Renaissance scholars to return to the original Greek and Latin source materials in their studies. The great humanist scholar Erasmus

(1466–1536) employed it as much as possible. In general, this is the method favored by most modern historians.

> *In my study of the development of modern political parties, I shall be using, AD FONTES, material from the national archives of the Democratic and Republican parties.*

ad hoc (Latin) (ad HOC) (adv.)
For this. Generally a makeshift solution to a problem, something that is unlikely to have general applicability.

> *Given the odd nature of our current situation, we'll have to create an AD HOC committee to propose solutions to the problem.*

ad hominem (Latin) (ad HOM-ih-nem) (adv.)
Literally, "to the man." In logical theory, it refers to a kind of argument that tries to attack another proposition by impugning the character of the person putting it forward. This is a logical fallacy.

> *Saying that the senator is a sexual pervert—although you may be accurate—is tantamount to launching an AD HOMINEM argument on him, since you can't refute his charges of political corruption.*

ad infinitum (Latin) (ad en-feh-NEE-toom) (adv.)
Literally, "to infinity." More usually, it means "from this point onward without ending." In other words, it refers to any event or sequence with no known ending.

> *The senator's speech was evidently intended to continue AD INFI-NITUM until his audience was converted to his point of view or died of boredom.*

adiós (Spanish) (ah-dee-OHSS) (interjection)
"We'll see you tomorrow." The standard Spanish farewell.

> *Let's get out of this place. ADIÓS, muchachos!*

ad libitum (Latin) (ad LEE-bih-toom) (adv.)
Literally, "at one's pleasure." It's often shortened to ad lib, which is the form in which most people hear it. Ad lib, in ordinary usage, has come to mean something that is done or said spontaneously, without rehearsal.

Many of the Marx Brothers' live performances were given AD LIBI-TUM; hence the legend that no two performances of Animal Crackers *were ever the same.*

ad litem (Latin) (ad LEE-tem) (adj.)
Acting in court on behalf of someone else who for some reason is unable to represent him- or herself. For example, an underage child on whose behalf a lawsuit is brought would be represented by another party—possibly a parent or guardian—who would be said to be acting ad litem.

Mr. Smith is representing Mrs. Smith, the plaintiff in the lawsuit, AD LITEM, since Mrs. Smith is in a coma and unable to speak for. herself.

ad nauseam (Latin) (ad NAW-zee-um) (adv.)
To the point of causing nausea. Although it is usually used concerning arguments that continue to a point that they're likely to make everyone involved throw up, it can also be more generally applied.

I find this children's Christmas pageant has continued AD NAU-SEAM, to the point where most of the audience is in a coma.

ad oculos (Latin) (ad OK-oo-lohss) (adv.)
By means of the eyes. Verified visually.

I might not have believed the existence of UFOs, had I not confirmed it AD OCULOS.

ad vitam aeternam (Latin) (ad WE-tahm eye-TER-nahm) (adj.)
Literally, "to eternal life." More generally, for all time, forever. It's also the name of a heavy metal band, if anyone's interested.

This party is stretching on AD VITAM AETERNAM. Why don't we go somewhere quiet and get a drink?

ad vitam aut culpam (Latin) (ad VEE-tahm out KUHL-pahm) (phrase)
"For life or until fault." This is a principle in Scottish law that guarantees an official (generally a judge) to hold office until such time as he commits an impeachable offense. In 1746, the Heritable Jurisdictions Act of the Scottish Parliament guaranteed a judge would hold his office in this manner once he had been in office for seven years. In general

conversation, it can refer to a more general principle that an official should be in office unless there is a legal reason to remove him or her.

> *The justices of the United States Supreme Court are appointed AD VITAM AUT CULPAM; an impeachment has occurred only once in the history of the institution.*

A

aetatis suae (Latin) (eye-TAH-tiss SOO-eye) (adj.)
Of his or her time. This expression often appears on old gravestones, where it takes the meaning of "in the year of his age," referring to the age at which the deceased died.

> *Sheila Jones passed from this life AETATIS SUAE 39.*

affaire de coeur (French) (a-FAIR deh KOOR) (noun)
Literally, an "affair of the heart." A love affair, usually one that is extramarital or in some other way tastes of scandal. The French enjoy this sort of thing, particularly when it happens to politicians. In America, we're scandalized when our politicians have mistresses; in Paris, people are scandalized when the premier doesn't.

> *The former congressman was forced to resign his office when it came to light that he had, while in Washington, engaged in an AFFAIRE DE COEUR involving a dominatrix, two cross-dressers, and a standard poodle.*

affaire d'honneur (French) (a-FAIR don-ur) (noun)
Literally, an "affair of honor." In practice, this refers to a duel, fought to settle an argument over honor. The French, being French, have a nice sense of propriety about such things, and there are elaborate rules governing the conduct of the seconds, the choice of weapons, and so on. In the eighteenth and nineteenth centuries, when such things were common, there were those who became experts on these ceremonies without, of course, ever directly being involved themselves.

> *The AFFAIRE D'HONNEUR between Alexander Hamilton and Aaron Burr, fought in Weehawken, New Jersey, in 1804, ended in the death of Hamilton, former U.S. Secretary of the Treasury.*

a fortiori (Latin) (ah for-tee-AWR-ree) (adv.)
A rhetorical term meaning "argument from the stronger reason." Generally, it refers to an argument that is strongly supported by

verifiable facts. The general implication is that the opposing argument is inherently weaker.

> *That nuclear war is bad is shown A FORTIORI by the fact that in the event of one occurring, most of the world's population would be dead.*

agent provocateur (French) (ah-ZHAUNT pro-vah-kah-TUR) (noun)

One who, acting secretly on behalf of other forces, infiltrates an organization and creates an incident that will allow his employers to attack those he has infiltrated. Such incidents are often violent, creating the impression that the organization in question is violent.

> *The Haymarket bombing incident in Chicago in 1886 in which eight police officers were killed was almost certainly the work of an AGENT PROVOCATEUR, seeking to give police an excuse to crush the nascent union movement.*

agnus dei (Latin) (AG-nuss DAY-ee) (noun)

The lamb of God. This expression first appears in the Gospel According to John, when John the Baptist cries, "Behold the Lamb of God who takes away the sin of the world" (John 1:29). The lamb is a widely used symbol in Christianity and finds expression in popular culture as one of the most widely eaten dishes at Easter. Although since Jesus was the Lamb of God, one might think it a bit strange to eat a lamb at the celebration of his resurrection.

> **Nota Bene**
> There has been considerable theological argument over the years about the sacrificial character of Jesus's crucifixion, and early Christians sometimes associated the Lamb of God with the ancient custom of a "scapegoat," a goat that would be sacrificed to atone for others' sins. St. Anselm of Canterbury, however, argued that Jesus's sacrifice was conscious and willing, and therefore he was not a scapegoat but a unique atonement for the sins of Mankind.

à la carte (French) (ah lah KART) (adj.)
Literally, "according to the menu," this refers to items that are sold separately. Other dishes are sold as packages, with side dishes included. Other menus offer complete meals at a fixed price (prix fixe).

Rather than the veal with scalloped potatoes, I'd like the veal À LA CARTE, please.

al dente (Italian) (ahl DEN-tay) (adj.)
Literally "to the tooth." A cooking term that specifies pasta (or, sometimes, rice or beans) should be cooked until it is no longer hard but still firm when bitten.

I prefer my pasta AL DENTE, not mushy the way it is in most American restaurants.

alea iacta est (Latin) (AL-ee-ah YAK-tah est) (phrase)
The die has been cast. This, according to the Roman historian Suetonius, (69–c. 130) was said by Julius Caesar (100 B.C.– 44 B.C.) when he crossed the Rubicon River in Northern Italy in 49 B.C. on his way to challenge Pompey (106 B.C.–48 B.C.) for control of Rome. From this incident, we also get the phrase "crossing the Rubicon," meaning to take an action from which there is no turning back.

> **Nota Bene**
> Julius Caesar (100 B.C.–44 B.C.) was among the most successful military commanders ever produced by Rome. Among other things, he pacified the Roman province of Gaul and invaded Britain, though his army withdrew without completely conquering the island. Caesar's return to Rome in 49 B.C. was the culmination of a period of civil war between various factions seeking to control the decaying Roman republic. Many feared that a triumphant Caesar would end the republic and return Rome to the monarchy, and for that reason a group of senators stabbed him to death on the floor of the senate in 44 B.C. Ironically, the long-term result of this murder was the rise of Caesar's nephew Octavian, who became Augustus, the first Roman emperor.

alfresco (Italian) (ahl-FRESS-ko) (adj.)
To eat outside, from the Italian for at fresh temperature. Alfresco dining was made popular in the cafés and trattorias of Europe. Today, many restaurants offer patrons the option of dining outside during the summer months.
It's such a lovely day; let's dine ALFRESCO.

Allah il Allah (Arabic) (AH-lah ill AH-lah) (phrase)
There is no god but God. This is part of the Shahahada, or testimony, that is an essential part of Islam. All Muslims must make a declaration of belief, part of the Five Pillars of Islam. In Arabic, it runs, *la 'ilaha 'illallah, Muhammad rasulu-llah* (there is no god but God and Mohammed is the messenger of God).

Allez! (French) (ah-LAY) (verb)
Go! Get out of here! Begone! The imperative form of the French verb *aller.*
I've got lots of work to do, and I don't have time to talk to you, so ALLEZ!

alter ego (Latin) (AHL-ter EE-go) (noun)
Another personality that is different from one's normal self. The term is also applied to a collection of personality traits that are exhibited apart from the way a person normally acts. The term has widespread use in literature, including in comic books, where a superhero's secret identity is sometimes referred to as his or her alter ego. For instance, Superman's alter ego is the mild-mannered Clark Kent. Spiderman is better known to his friends and family as the nebbish Peter Parker.
He's usually such a nice person, but he was so mean today. It's as if we encountered his ALTER EGO.

Nota Bene
Created by Jerry Siegel and Joe Shuster in 1932, Superman has been seen by many as the quintessential American hero. Gifted with superpowers by his origins on the now-destroyed planet Krypton, Superman fights for Earth, his adopted home, guarding it against both internal threats (such as master criminal Lex Luthor) and external perils. At the same time, writers for Superman quickly figured out

that a character who couldn't be injured or face any appreciable danger was pretty boring, so over the years they've kept coming up with weaknesses—in a rewrite of the series in 1986, it transpired, for example, that Superman has to hold his breath while flying through outer space.

alter ipse amicus (Latin) (AHL-tare IP-say ah-ME-kuss) (expression)
A friend is another self. A lovely sentiment for a friendship card.

amicus curiae (Latin) (ah-ME-kiss COOR-ee-eye) (noun)
Friend of the court. Someone not directly involved in a court case who offers information or an opinion designed to influence the case's outcome. Generally it takes the form of a legal brief, which is taken into consideration by the presiding judge but does not have to be admitted into evidence.
> *The American Civil Liberties Union has filed numerous AMICUS CURIAE briefs in cases involving civil rights.*

amor patriae (Latin) (AH-more PAH-tree-eye) (noun)
Love of one's country; patriotism
> *A politician should have no higher sentiment than AMOR PATRIAE; sadly, most of them love money more than their country.*

Amor vincit omnia (Latin) (AH-more WIN-kit AHM-nee-ah) (phrase)
Love conquers all. In Chaucer's *The Canterbury Tales*, the Prioress is described as having
> *"A string of beads and gauded all with green;*
> *And therefrom hung a brooch of golden sheen*
> *Whereon there was first written a crowned 'A,'*
> *And under, Amor vincit omnia."*

A somewhat odd sentiment, perhaps, for someone who has given her life to the church.

amour propre (French) (ah-MOOR PRO-pre) (noun)
Self-esteem; self-love. Jean-Jacques Rousseau (1712–1778) argued that this kind of self-esteem depended on the good opinions of oth-

ers. He contrasted this with *amour de soi*, which was self-love without any external support.

> *His insults have not affected my AMOUR PROPRE, since I know he's an idiot.*

ancien régime (French) (ahn-SIEN ray-ZHEEM) (noun)

Literally, "ancient regime" or "ancient monarchy." It refers to the government and social system of France from the fifteenth to the eighteenth century. The most outstanding representative of this system was Louis XIV, the Sun King, who built the magnificent palace of Versailles as a kind of physical monument to the *ancien régime*. The regime perished in the French Revolution, and, despite attempts by Napoleon and Louis Napoleon to resurrect it, it remained dead.

angst (German) (ahnkst) (noun)
Fear, anxiety, turmoil. Although the word is an old one, it came into widespread use in the late nineteenth and early twentieth centuries, during the rise of the cultural movement called modernism. This reflected the underlying nervousness of Western society, which became intensified after the First World War.

> *The ANGST of modern man is reflected in Edvard Munch's famous painting, "The Scream."*

anno Domini (Latin) (AHN-no DOH-min-ee) (adj.)
Literally, "the year of our Lord." It refers to dates occurring after the supposed incarnation of Christ. It was invented in the sixth century by the Greek monk Dionysius Exiguus and popularized by the English historian the Venerable Bede in his *Historia Ecclesiastica Gentis Anglorum*. In more recent years, it has been replaced by Common Era, or C.E., and Before Common Era, or B.C.E.

> *I wrote this book in 2011 ANNO DOMINI.*

anno regni (Latin) (AHN-no REG-nee) (adj.)
In the year of (his or her) reign. This system of dating depends on the regnal year of a particular king or queen. It is almost never used—not least because there are so few kings and queens anymore (at least ones we pay much attention to).

The wedding of Prince William and Catherine Middleton occurred in ANNO REGNI 59.

A

annus horribilis (Latin) (AHN-nus hor-EE-bi-liss) (noun)
Year of horrors. The phrase was used by Queen Elizabeth II in 1992 in a speech. From her point of view, it was certainly not a great year. In March, the separation of the Duke and Duchess of York was announced. In April, Princess Anne divorced her husband. In November, the royal residence Windsor Castle caught fire, and in December, Prince Charles and Princess Diana announced they were separating.

1992 is not a year on which I shall look back with undiluted pleasure. In the words of one of my more sympathetic correspondents, it has turned out to be an ANNUS HORRIBILIS.
—Queen Elizabeth II

annus mirabilis (Latin) (AHN-nus mir-AH-bi-liss) (noun)
Wonderful year. It is also the title of a poem by the English writer John Dryden. He was referring to the year 1666, although it wasn't a great year for many people; the Great Fire of London wiped out a large chunk of the city, and England was revisited by the Plague. Dryden didn't contract the disease, so from his point of view it wasn't a bad year, all things considered.

Some might say that the last year before the financial crisis, 2007, was a kind of ANNUS MIRABILIS.

antebellum (Latin) (AN-tee-BELL-um) (adj.)
Literally, "before the war." Specifically, this term is used to refer to the United States prior to the Civil War (1861–1865), especially to the South and to prewar Southern culture.

Because of the destructive character of the Civil War, only a few ANTEBELLUM houses are still standing in Georgia.

ante mortem (Latin) (AN-tee MORE-tem) (adj.)
Before death. Often used in coroners' reports and other medical documents.

All indications are that the bruises on the subject's neck were produced ANTE MORTEM, indicating he was probably strangled by an unknown person or persons.

aperçu (French) (ah-per-SOO) (noun)
A clever insight; alternately, a summation.
I find your APERÇU of the situation to be extremely helpful.

apéritif (French) (ah-per-i-TEEF) (noun)
A predinner drink, designed to stimulate the palate in preparation for the meal. Its counterpart is a digestif, which is served at the meal's conclusion.
Excuse me, would you care for an APÉRITIF before we go in to dinner?

> **Nota Bene**
> The American version of the apéritif is the cocktail, invented in the early nineteenth century (it is first mentioned in *The Farmer's Cabinet* in 1803). Cocktails became particularly widely known during Prohibition in the 1920s, when they were considered a mark of the sophisticated New York culture that flourished in places such as the Algonquin Hotel.

a posse ad esse (Latin) (ah POSS-ay ad ESS-ay) (phrase)
Literally, "From possibility to reality." The general point is that it's an impermissible step to assume that because something is a possibility, it must, therefore, be a reality.
Although I admit the possibility of a purple winged cow, A POSSE AD ESSE I require more proof before I admit its existence.

> **Nota Bene**
> A somewhat longer version of the previous phrase is *a posse ad esse non valet consequentia,* which translates as, "From a thing's possibility, you can't be certain of its reality."

a posteriori (Latin) (ah poss-tair-ee-OH-ree) (adv.)
From later. A philosophical term that refers to knowledge gained from experience or empirical evidence.
That a hot stove will burn you if you touch it is something I discovered A POSTERIORI.

A

apparatchik (Russian) (a-par-AHT-chik) (noun)
This Russian term for a bureaucrat was particularly applied from
1917 to 1989 to members of the Communist Party in the Soviet
Union who held government positions and so were seen as function-
aries. The image of the typical apparatchik was of someone who was
so immersed in details as to lose sight of any sort of larger picture.
*I spent all last Saturday arguing with some APPARATCHIK from
the DMV about whether I need my original birth certificate to get a
driver's license.*

après moi, le deluge (French) (AH-pray MWAH le de-LOOZH) (phrase)
After me, the flood. This saying is doubtfully attributed to the
French monarch Louis XV (1710–1774) and apparently predicted
the chaos that would lead to the French Revolution of 1789 and
the overthrow of the monarchy. Given the disastrous character of
Louis's reign (he damaged the country's reputation abroad and
almost bankrupted its treasury) he may well have had an idea that
things would go badly after his death. Today, it is used to predict
any oncoming period of decline and disaster.

a priori (Latin) (ah pri-O-ree) (adv.)
Refers to knowledge gained independent of experience. A priori
information is just "known" and cannot be verified or disproved. The
philosopher Immanuel Kant (1704–1824) made the study of the difference between a priori and a posteriori knowledge his life's work.
We intuit the existence of a higher being A PRIORI.

à propos (French) (ah pro-POH) (adv.)
At the right time, appropriately.
*Since we're discussing budgets, this is an À PROPOS time to bring
up the question of salary raises for the staff.*

aqua vitae (Latin) (AH-kwah WE-tie) (noun)
Although it was taken, for a long time, to refer to the miraculous
power of water in the baptismal ceremony, it came to mean alcohol,
specifically distilled alcohol used in beverages.
*The sun is over the yardarm somewhere, so it's time for us to indulge
in a little AQUA VITAE.*

> **Nota Bene**
> Whiskey, among the most important uses of aqua vitae, derives its name from the Scottish Gaelic term *uisge beatha*, meaning "water of life." The first written record concerning it appears in the *Annals of Clonmacnoise*, compiled in 1405.

aquila non capit muscas (Latin) (ah-KEE-la non KAA-pit MOOS-kass) (saying)
Literally, "An eagle doesn't catch flies." Meaning that someone who's important shouldn't concern herself with unimportant questions but instead leave those to lesser persons.

> **Nota Bene**
> Eagles had an important symbolic meaning to the Romans. They were omens of good fortune, and the Roman legions carried a representation of an eagle into battle. One of the greatest of all Roman military disasters occurred in A.D. 9 when an alliance of Germanic tribes attacked and slaughtered three legions in the Teutoburg Forest, capturing their eagle symbols. The Emperor Augustus was horrified at the event and was seen by his contemporaries occasionally banging his head against the wall and appealing to the gods, "Give me back my eagles!"

arbiter elegantiarum (Latin) (AR-bi-tare el-ay-gan-tee-AH-rum) (noun)
Someone who is a recognized authority on matters of taste, particularly fashion.
> *As a result of the television show* What Not to Wear, *Stacy London has become a widely respected ARBITER ELEGANTIARUM, together with her co-star Clinton Kelly.*

armoire (French) (ar-MWAHR) (noun)
A large cabinet for storing clothing, what in English would be called a wardrobe. Today most armoires include several sets of drawers,

though this was not always the case. The earliest versions were probably merely chests in which extra clothing was folded and packed away until needed.

> *Because the weather is turning warm, I've put all my winter coats in the ARMOIRE until next fall.*

arrivederci (Italian) (ah-reev-ah-DARE-chee) (salutation)
Goodbye, so long.

> *Until we see you next year, ARRIVEDERCI!*

ars gratia artis (Latin) (arz GRAH-tee-ah AR-tiss) (motto)
Art for art's sake. The motto of Metro-Goldwyn-Mayer, appearing in the circle above the head of the roaring lion (named Leo). In the nineteenth century, it was the slogan of an artistic movement called the Aesthetics, who believed that art had no inherent value outside of its depiction of beauty. Oscar Wilde, a leading Aesthete, remarked, "All art is quite useless."

Ars longa vita brevis (Latin) (arz LONG-ah WE-tah BRE-wiss) (phrase)
Art is long, life is short. Originally an aphorism by the Greek physician Hippocrates, it is often interpreted to mean that because our lives are fleeting, we should enjoy the aesthetic pleasure we derive from a work of art, which will outlive us. Keeping in mind that Hippocrates was a physician and that in the original Greek, the word "ars" probably meant "craft," it seems clear that what Hippocrates was getting at was that because life is fragile, a doctor should know what he's doing before he does it—a strong caution for today's physicians.

au contraire (French) (oh con-TRAIR) (adv.)
To the contrary.

> *AU CONTRAIRE, sir, I don't find your joke about my height in the least amusing.*

au courant (French) (oh coor-AWNT) (adv.)
Current, up to date.

> *I remain AU COURANT through my perusal of the New York Times and the Boston Globe every morning.*

au fait (French) (oh fay) (adv.)
Fully informed.
> *The president, because of his excellent sources of information, has remained AU FAIT regarding the developing situation in the Middle East.*

Aufgeschoben ist nicht aufgehoben (German) (owf-ge-SHOW-ben ist nikt owf-ge-HO-ben) (phrase)
Put off does not mean giving up. A phrase that should offer comfort to those of us given to terminal procrastination.

auf Wiedersehen (German) (owf VEE-der-sane) (interjection)
Farewell.
> *In* The Sound of Music *(1965), the children of Captain von Trapp bid their father's ball guests AUF WIEDERSEHEN in a song that outdoes just about every other number in the film for sentimental sloppiness.*

au gratin (French) (oh grah-TAN) (adj.)
In cooking, a dish topped with bread crumbs and cheese. The food is then placed under a broiler to give the topping a rich golden brown color.
> *I just made macaroni and cheese AU GRATIN, using panko instead of regular bread crumbs.*

au mieux (French) (oh myuh) (adv.)
On the best terms; on terms of intimacy.
> *Despite our divorce, my ex-husband and I have remained AU MIEUX.*

au naturel (French) (oh na-tur-ELLE) (adj.)
Nude, naked. It's sometimes used in cooking to mean without any sort of garnish, but it's a lot more fun to use it with the other meaning.
> *My girlfriend and I hung out at the beach last weekend, and since there was no one around, we were AU NATUREL.*

au revoir (French) (oh reh-VWAHR) (salutation)
Literally, "Until we meet again." Goodbye.

At the end of P. L. Travers's classic children's novel Mary Poppins, *the children notice that when the magical nanny bids them farewell, she says* AU REVOIR. *From this they deduce that she'll be back someday.*

Aut amat aut odit mulier, nihil est tertium (Latin) (owt ah-MAHT owt OH-dit moo-lee-air ni-hill est TARE-tee-um) (phrase) A woman either loves or hates, there is no third way. A saying from the Roman poet and playwright Publilius Syrus (1st century B.C.). The quotation is from his *Sententiae*, the only one of his works that remains in existence.

> **Nota Bene**
> Roman drama drew heavily on Greek traditions. The most famous Roman playwrights, Terence (190–159 B.C.) and Plautus (254–184 B.C.), created plays that relied on the principles established by their Greek predecessors. Although the Romans enjoyed plays, relatively few seem to have been written during the period of empire, and Roman audiences evidently fell back on the old Greek standards.

aut Caesar aut nihil (Latin) (awt KAI-zahr awt NEE-hill) (phrase) Caesar or nothing. More generally, either a principled position or nothing. This phrase was adopted by the Renaissance prince Cesare Borgia (1475–1507) as a personal motto.

> **Nota Bene**
> Cesare Borgia was the quintessential Renaissance prince. The inspiration for Machiavelli's *The Prince*, he was a general, statesman, and effective ruler of the Papal States during the Renaissance. He died while fighting for King John III of Navarre. Far more mythologized during his death than he had been celebrated in life, he remains the inspiration for modern morality-challenged figures such as Henry Kissinger.

auto da fé (Spanish) (aw toh dah FAY) (phrase).
Burning at the stake, although the original meaning was concerned with the professing of public penitence made by the vic-
tims. Eventually the term came to be associated with the worst
excesses of the Spanish Inquisition. Generally, the ritual involved
a reading of the sentences of those charged with heresy, followed
by their execution.

autres temps, autres moeurs (French) (OH-tre TEMP OH-tre
morez) (phrase)
Other times, other customs. More generally, whatever people may
have done at other times, this is what we do now. Possibly originated in the writings of Chrétien de Troyes, the twelfth-century
composer of Arthurian romances.

aut vincere aut mori (Latin) (awt WIN-kay-re awt MOR-ree)
(phrase)
To conquer or to die. More loosely, Victory or death!
We can't possibly do anything more to win this football game. AUT
VINCERE AUT MORI!

avant-garde (French) (AH-vant gard) (noun)
Literally, "advance guard." Cultural movement in Europe, primarily
in France, that was marked by an embrace of the new and daring.
Subsequently, it has come to mean anything that pushes the boundaries of accepted taste.
Rap music has become the AVANT-GARDE of modern musical
style.

avec plaisir (French) (ah-VEK play-ZEER) (interjection)
With pleasure.
It would be a privilege to open the door for you. AVEC PLAISIR!

ave Imperator, morituri te salutant (Latin) (AH-way im-per-
AH-tor mor-ee-TOO-ree tay sa-LOO-tant) (phrase)
Hail, Emperor! We who are about the die, salute thee! The supposed phrase with which gladiators in the Roman arenas greeted
the emperor. One is invited to wonder whether this was, in fact,
their sentiment, since most of them would die in the next thirty

or forty minutes, and those who survived were likely to do so with severe wounds. Some few benefited from the Roman games, though, and won their freedom from enslavement.

Ave Maria (Latin) (AH-way Mar-EE-ah)
The beginning of the traditional Catholic prayer asking for the intercession of the Virgin Mary. The prayer has been set to music on many occasions, and it forms the basis of an important section of the Catholic liturgy.

> **Nota Bene**
> The original basis of Hail Mary was the episode in the Gospel According to Luke in which an angel of the Lord appeared to Mary of Nazareth, saying, "Hail, Mary, full of grace, the Lord is with thee." This became an essential part of the cult of the Virgin Mary, which was a significant element of the Middle Ages and the Renaissance, both in literature and art.

"Life is a foreign language:
all men mispronounce it."

—Christopher Morley

B

B

baksheesh (Farsi) (bahk-SHEESH) (noun)
Tipping or charitable giving. In recent years, it has also come to mean bribing or otherwise gaining political influence.

> *I wouldn't have any influence at all with our congressman if it weren't for the BAKSHEESH that I spread around during his last campaign.*

basta (Spanish) (BAHS-tah) (interjection)
Enough!

> *I'm tired of eating nothing but tapas and drinking sherry. BASTA!*

beaucoup (French) (boh-COO) (interjection)
Much.

> *Last night's party was filled with BEAUCOUP wine, dancing, and song. Unfortunately, I'm paying the price for that this morning.*

beau geste (French) (boh zhest) (noun)
A noble gesture that is empty of substance.

Nota Bene
Beau Geste is the title of a 1924 adventure novel by P. C. Wren. It was later made into a movie with Gary Cooper in the lead role. The story concerns the theft of a precious jewel, forcing Beau Geste, an upper-class Briton, to enlist in the French Foreign Legion, where he dies valiantly. It's revealed that he concealed the theft of the gem for honorable reasons and thus becomes the embodiment of the ethos Englishmen liked to think drove the British empire.

---

beau monde (French) (boh mond) (noun)
High society. The phrase reflects the highly class-ridden society of Western Europe prior to the end of World War I.

> *We were members of the BEAU MONDE before 1918, but afterwards we settled into the upper ranks of the bourgeoisie.*

bel esprit (French) (bell eh-SPREE) (noun)
Someone who is highly intelligent and cultivated. Not unlike the compilers of this book.

> *I've always looked upon a person like Joan Didion as a BEL ESPRIT.*

belles-lettres (French) (bell-LET-re) (noun)
Well-written, well-regarded literature. Classic literature.
> *The works of Victor Hugo and Honoré de Balzac are taken, often, as epitomes of French BELLES-LETTRES.*

bête noir (French) (BEHT nwahr) (noun)
Antagonist. Chosen enemy. One who is a persistent challenge or foe.
> *Someone who is openly foolish has always been my BÊTE NOIR, but I've managed to survive many such people.*

Bildungsroman (German) (bill-dungs-ROH-mahn) (noun)
A term of literary criticism, this refers to a coming-of-age story that shows the growth of the protagonist through the various stages of adolescence, teen angst, and early youth. The Germans were particularly struck with this kind of thing and produced bales of these novels in the nineteenth and early twentieth centuries.
> *Goethe's* The Sorrows of Young Werther *is a classic BILDUNG-SROMAN of the German Romantic period.*

billet doux (French) (bill-ay DOO) (noun)
A love letter.
> *Because I knew that Susan had a major crush on Robert, I agreed to carry a BILLET DOUX between them—although it made me throw up a little in my mouth.*

Bis dat qui cito dat (Latin) (biss daht kwi KEE-to dat) (phrase)
That which is given quickly is twice given. In other words, if you donate something without really considering it, your gift is more generous. There's no indication of the source of this popular Latin proverb.

Bis vincit, qui se vincit in victoria (Latin) (bis win-kit KWI say win-kit in wik-TOH-ree-ah) (phrase)
He conquers twice who, in the hour of his conquest, conquers himself. The general meaning is that the greatest generals are those who exercise self-restraint, a deeply Roman virtue.

Blitzkrieg (German) (BLITZ-kreeg) (noun)
Literally, "lightning war." A term applied to the German strategy during the first part of World War II of attacking swiftly and

ruthlessly. The Germans launched blitzkriegs against Poland, Belgium, France, and, in 1941, Russia—though in the latter case it didn't work out too well for them.

> *Given the filthy state of your apartment, I've launched a cleaning BLITZKREIG. Did you know you had a floor under those piles of dirty clothes, books, magazines, and something disgusting that I had to remove with a pair of old kitchen tongs?*

B

bona fides (Latin) (BON-ah feeds) (adj.)
Good faith.

> *When I went to dinner with my ex-spouse, I brought a check for six months' back child support, as evidence of my BONA FIDES.*

bon mot (French) (bohn moh) (noun)
Literally, "a good word." A witticism, something said cleverly.

> *At the sort of parties I'm often forced to attend, intellectuals stand around sipping white wine and nibbling brie, dropping BON MOTS all over the place. It's enough to make you want to throw up.*

bonne chance (French) (bohn SHAHNSS) (interjection)
Good luck! Often used with a slightly ironical tone.

> *I see you've placed all your money on the possibility of winning the Grand Slam lottery. BONNE CHANCE!*

Bon repas doit commencer par la faim (French) (bon ray-PAH dwah koh-moh-SAY par lah FAHM) (phrase)
French saying, literally, "A good meal should begin with hunger." More generally, if you're hungry, you'll enjoy a good meal more.

bon vivant (French) (bohn vee-VAHN) (noun)
Someone who enjoys life. A gourmet.

> *I liked Jean because he believed in partying until 2 A.M. He was, in fact, a BON VIVANT.*

boychik (Yiddish) (BOY-chik) (noun)
Term of affection for a young man.

> *Such a good BOYCHIK he is then. So handsome, and he loves his mother!*

Brevis ipsa vita est sed malis fit longior (Latin) (BREH-wiss IP-sa WE-ta est said MAH-liss fit LONG-ee-or) (quotation)
Our life is short but made longer by misfortunes. Attributed to Publilius Syrus (1st century B.C.)

Brevissima ad divitias per contemptum divitiarum via est (Latin) (breh-WISS-ih-mah ad dee-WEE-tee-ass pare con-TEMP-toom dee-wee-tee-AR-oom WE-ah- est) (quotation)
The shortest road to wealth is the contempt of wealth. Attributed to Seneca the Younger (4 B.C.–A.D. 65)

B

> **Nota Bene**
> Seneca the Younger (so called to distinguish him from his father, Seneca the Elder) was a Roman philosopher and playwright who was the tutor of the Emperor Nero. Seneca was an exponent of Stoicism, which was among the most popular philosophies in Rome. Stoics argued that strong emotions were to be avoided, since they inevitably led to errors in judgment. Seneca and his followers added that virtue is the only thing necessary for happiness, an idea that sat well with Roman emperors, who didn't practice austerity themselves but strongly encouraged it among their subjects.

bubbala (Yiddish) (BOO-buh-luh) (noun)
A term of affection, particularly applied by an older person to a younger one.
> *Come in and sit down, BUBBALA. Are you hungry? Sit. I'll fix you something to nosh on.*

bwana (Swahili) (BWAH-na) (noun)
Boss, important person. In Hollywood movies, this was the way in which African natives invariably addressed white explorers, regardless of whether the Africans were supposed to be native Swahili speakers. Writers were, perhaps, unaware that the term does not always have a favorable connotation in Swahili.
> *Don't go down that path, BWANA! Lions will eat you. Oh, wait . . . never mind. It's okay. Go down that path. No problem!*

"There is the fear, common to all English-only speakers, that the chief purpose of foreign languages is to make fun of us. Otherwise, you know, why not just come out and say it?"

—Barbara Ehrenreich

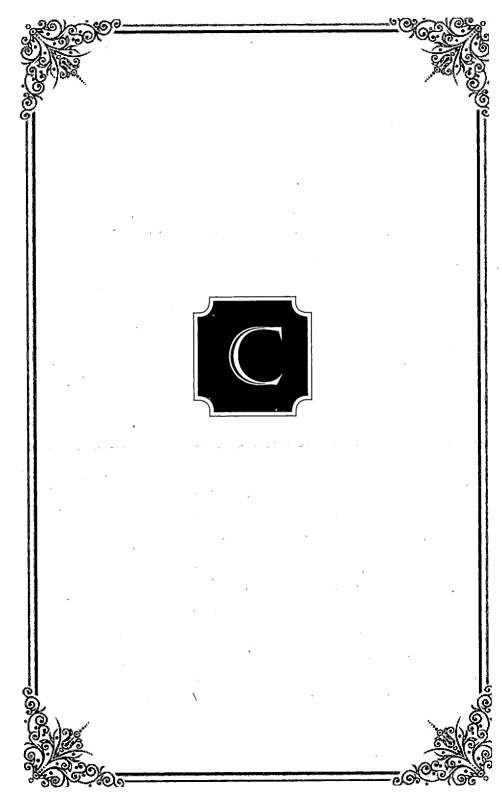

camera obscura (Latin) (KA-mer-ah ob-SKUR-ah) (noun)
An early version of a slide projector, this device projects an image of its surroundings on a screen. Like many devices, this seems to have been invented in China, where it's mentioned as early as the fifth century b.c. Euclid (c. 300 B.C.) was aware of it, as was Aristotle (384–322 B.C.). Eventually, it led to the discovery of photography in the nineteenth century.

ça ne fait rien (French) (SAH ne FAY ree-EHN) (phrase)
Literally, "It makes nothing." Colloquially, never mind.
I don't mind that you've obviously not been listening to me for the past ten minutes. ÇA NE FAIT RIEN.

caput mortuum (Latin) (KA-put MOR-too-oom) (noun)
Literally, "dead head." The worthless remains of something. The term was used in alchemy, the medieval "science" of transmuting base metals into others (particularly gold). *Caput mortuum* is also the term for a bright purple pigment, used in oil paints and dyes and associated with royal personages (hence the English term "assume the purple," meaning to ascend to higher office).
I've concluded an experiment in which I evaporated sea water, leaving a CAPUT MORTUUM of salt.

Carpe diem (Latin) (KAR-pay DEE-em) (interjection)
Seize the day. Originally a phrase from a poem by Horace (65 B.C.–8 B.C.), the term became associated with a group of seventeenth-century poets known as the Metaphysicals. They included particularly Robert Herrick (1591–1674) who expressed this sentiment in his poem "To the Virgins, to Make Much of Time."
Gather ye rosebuds while ye may,
Old Time is still a-flying;
And this same flower that smiles today,
Tomorrow will be dying.

> **Nota Bene**
> *Carpe diem!* was the theme of the 1989 film *Dead Poets Society*, starring Robert Sean Leonard and Robin Williams. Williams played a private school teacher who sought to inspire his students to seize the day. He didn't read to them from the Metaphysical poets, but rather from the Romantics, such as Byron, Shelley, and Keats, who also practiced a philosophy of *carpe diem*. In the end, given that the film was set in the 1950s, conformity and mediocrity triumph over romanticism, although a young Ethan Hawke has the last word, while standing on top of his desk in the classroom.

C

carte blanche (French) (kart blahnsh) (noun)
Literally, "white card." Colloquially, permission to do anything. In English, this is sometimes expressed as "being given a blank check."
> *As far as I'm concerned, you have CARTE BLANCHE as far as what kind of car you want to buy for me.*

Carthago delenda est (Latin) (kar-TAH-go day-LEN-da est) (quotation)
Carthage must be destroyed. The city of Carthage (located roughly at the site of the present-day Tunis) was a long-time enemy of Rome. The two cities fought three wars, known as the Punic Wars, and in all of them Rome was victorious. During the period leading up to the last war, the Roman statesman Cato the Elder (234 B.C.–149 B.C.) would end all his speeches to the Senate with this slogan. After the Battle of Carthage in 146 B.C., the city was, indeed, destroyed and its site sown with salt so nothing would ever grow there again. The slogan was later deployed by others to suggest a national imperative that cannot be avoided.

casus belli (Latin) (KASS-us BELL-ee) (noun)
The cause for war. The reason a war was (or is) fought.
> *The CASUS BELLI for the American Civil War was slavery, though some have argued it was primarily the issue of states rights.*

causa mortis (Latin) (KOW-ssa MOR-tiss) (noun)
In contemplation of coming death. A gift that is given by someone who anticipates imminent death is said to be given for this reason. Generally speaking, if the giver of the gift doesn't actually die, she or he can hold on to the gift.

> *This fountain pen is very special to me, since my grandfather presented it to me CAUSA MORTIS when he had cancer.*

cause célèbre (French) (kohz say-LEB-re) (noun)
A notable case or cause. In particular, a court case that attracts a great deal of media or is important for its legal consequences . . . or both.

> *The murder trial of O. J. Simpson was a peculiarly American CAUSE CÉLÈBRE, with its intermixture of violence and scandal, racial overtones, and a circuslike atmosphere in the courtroom.*

Caveat emptor (Latin) (KAH-way-aht EMPT-or) (phrase)
Buyer beware. What businesses say to protect themselves from consumer lawsuits over defective products or services.

> *To your charge that I sold you a car whose engine had been replaced with one from a 1956 Edsel, I reply CAVEAT EMPTOR.*

Cave canem (Latin) (KAH-way KAH-nem) (phrase)
Beware of the dog. The counterpart for felines would be *cave cattem*, but for some reason one rarely sees this on signs outside people's houses.

C'est la guerre! (French) (say lah GAYR) (phrase)
Literally, "That is war." More generally, these are the kinds of things that happen in war.

> *It's a pity that those three villages were destroyed and their inhabitants massacred, but C'EST LA GUERRE.*

C'est la vie! (French) (say lah VEE) (phrase)
That's life. An expression of general resignation at the essential irrational and unfair character of the world.

> *I'm sorry that you lost your job and are being divorced by your wife while I just won $20 million in the lottery, but C'EST LA VIE! And no, I won't lend you any money.*

ceteris paribus (Latin) (KET-air-ees PAR-i-boos) (phrase)
Literally, "with other things the same." More colloquially, other things being equal. Most scientific experiments take place under an assumption of *ceteris paribus*, since scientists look for general laws rather than the specific phenomena of each particular event.

We can say, CETERIS PARIBUS, that water will boil at 212 degrees Fahrenheit.

Chacun à son gout (French) (SHA-con ah son GOO) (phrase)
To each his own taste. This phrase has been doubtfully attributed to Voltaire (1694–1778); certainly it expresses the great Frenchman's view that one shouldn't attempt to impose one's tastes and standards on others.

Personally, I loathe the taste of lobster, but CHACUN À SON GOUT.

cherchez la femme (French) (SHARE-shay lah FEM) (phrase)
Search for the woman. More generally, be on the lookout for girls—usually as a motive force for something, be it a quarrel, a crime, or some other event. For French men, this is one of the guiding principles of life, the other being that there's no occasion that won't be improved by a glass (or several) of wine. And what's wrong with that?

We're going to hit the clubs tonight; remember, CHERCHEZ LA FEMME.

chez nous (French) (SHAY new) (noun)
Where we live. Our personal domicile.

I'd like to invite you CHEZ NOUS for drinks this evening. Say about 8 o'clock.

chiaroscuro (Italian) (kee-ah-roh-SKOO-roh) (noun)
A technique much used in Italian painting of the seventeenth century in which light and dark were dramatically contrasted. The painter Caravaggio (1571–1610) was a master of this style, and it can be seen to good effect in such paintings as "The Calling of St. Matthew" and "The Crucifixion of St. Peter."

Caravaggio's paintings show the powerful interaction between their subjects through his use of CHIAROSCURO, which focuses our attention on the central actors in the drama.

chutzpah (Yiddish) (HOOTS-pah) (noun)
Boldness or nerve. It's occasionally good but often used negatively.
> *I can't believe he had the CHUTZPAH to tell his wife her new bathing suit made her look fat. I wonder how much he'll be left with after the divorce settlement.*

C

cinéma vérité (French) (SIN-a-mah VAY-ree-tay) (noun)
A style of filmmaking that uses naturalistic techniques as well as classic cinematic styles. Although the movement began among French filmmakers in the 1950s and 1960s, it has gained adherents around the world.
> *In America, Barbara Kopple's film* Harlan County U.S.A. *was an example of CINÉMA VÉRITÉ, with its unflinching examination of a strike by coal miners and the violence that erupted in its wake in Harlan County, Kentucky.*

circa (Latin) (SIR-ka) (adv.)
Around; about. Generally used to qualify a date that is not specifically known.
> *The Latin poet Publilius Syrus lived CIRCA the first century B.C.*

Cogito ergo sum (Latin) (KOG-ee-toh AIR-go soom) (quotation)
I think, therefore I am. The most famous quotation associated with the philosopher René Descartes (1596–1650). Descartes endeavored to develop a philosophy based on absolute skepticism of everything. Having tried to doubt everything possible, he concluded that the one thing he could not doubt was that he himself was doing the doubting. Therefore, the proof of his existence was his ability to contemplate the problem of his existence. From this, he proceeded to develop his philosophy, which is expressed in his book *Discourse on Method.*

cognoscenti (Latin) (kog-no-SENT-ee) (noun)
Those who are especially well informed and well read about a particular subject or subjects. Alternately, someone with a superior intellect. In other words, the kind of person the reader of this book aspires to be.

The fact that I'm a member of the COGNOSCENTI can be discerned by my easy command of a range of foreign language terms—all of which I memorized before this party in order to impress everyone.

coitus interruptus (Latin) (KOH-i-tuss in-tare-UP-tiss) (noun)
Interrupted or uncompleted sexual intercourse. It's sometimes been suggested as a birth-control method, although, all things considered, it's hard to think of one more likely to fail.

C

My companion and I experienced COITUS INTERRUPTUS last night when we got a little too enthusiastic and the bed collapsed under us.

comédie humaine (French) (KOH-may-dee oo-MAIN) (noun)
Loosely, the human condition, implying that our lives all contain an element of absurdity. *La Comédie Humaine* was the title of a collection of tales and novels by Honoré de Balzac (1799–1850) concerning French life in the period immediately after the end of Napoleonic rule.

As I grow older, I prefer to sit back and watch the COMÉDIE HUMAINE and laugh at the folly of others.

comme ci, comme ça (French) (kom SEE kom SAH) (phrase)
Literally, "Like this, like that." More generally, so-so or okay.

My day isn't too bad so far. COMME CI, COMME ÇA. We'll see what it's like after my interview with the boss this afternoon.

comme il faut (French) (kom eel FOE) (adv.)
According to the proper standards; accepted.

Those shoes you were wearing this morning were awful! Completely inappropriate. The ones you have on now are COMME IL FAUT for the sort of party we're going to.

Nota Bene
The French are fiercely jealous of the purity of their language. French traditionalists have long lamented the importation of such abominations as *le coca-cola* and *les cocktails*. To guard against this sort of invasion, the Académie Française was established by Cardinal Richelieu in 1635 and for the past three and three-quarter centuries has been fighting the good fight to keep French the way it was in the seventeenth century.

communibus locis (Latin) (kom-MOO-ni-boos LO-kiss) (noun)
In common places; that is to say, some relationship between several
places.

> *One finds intra-party strife in parliaments IN COMMUNIBUS
> LOCIS—whether in Paris, London, or Berlin.*

¿Como estas? (Spanish) (ko-mo ess-TASS) (interjection)
How's it going? How are you? Among the most common greetings
in Spanish.

> *Hey, buddy! ¿COMO ESTAS? Long time no see!*

compos mentis (Latin) (KOM-poss MEN-tiss) (adj.)
Of sound mind. Sane. The opposite is, naturally, non compos mentis. Though the term is a legal one, it's fallen into general usage.

> *Despite my client's claim to be a parakeet during the mating sea-
> son, I ask the court to regard him as COMPOS MENTIS. After
> all, you'll all notice the brightly colored sweater he's wearing in an
> effort to attract a mate.*

contemptus mundi (Latin) (kon-TEM-tuss MUN-dee) (phrase)
Scorn for the world. Rejection of the material world and its ben-
efits. This idea runs through much of ancient philosophy, particularly the Stoics, who believed that only virtue brings happiness.
This idea can also be found in the Latin phrase **vanitas vanitatem**,
usually translated, "Vanity, vanity, all is vanity."

> *Since losing my lottery winnings in Las Vegas, I have developed a
> CONTEMPTUS MUNDI and now seek to gratify myself through
> spiritual growth and exploration.*

contra mundum (Latin) (KON-tra MUN-dum) (adv.)
Against the world. Contrary to popular belief and opinion.

> *Galileo, CONTRA MUNDUM, held that the earth moves around
> the sun. Although he was forced by the church to recant his position,
> he never entirely abandoned it.*

corpus delicti (Latin) (KOR-puss day-LIK-tee) (noun)
Literally, "Body of crime." This is the principle that before someone
can be convicted of committing a crime, it must be proven that a
crime was, in fact, committed. The problem arises particularly in

murder cases in which no body of the victim is found. In such a case, the police and prosecution must prove to the court that there is an overwhelming likelihood of the missing person having been murdered.

The difficulty in the case of many missing people is to establish CORPUS DELICTI so that someone can be charged with murder.

corrigendum (Latin) (kor-i-GEN-doom) (noun)
A printer's error that is corrected or should be corrected. The plural is *corrigenda* (such errors are also sometimes referred to as *errata*).

I've sent my publisher a list of CORRIGENDA that must be fixed before the next edition of my book appears.

cosa nostra (Italian) (KOHSS-a NOSS-tra) (noun)
Literally, "our thing." The term was originally used to refer to Mafia originating in Sicily but has come to generally mean any form of Mafia, including those that come from other parts of Italy. The phrase was used by members of the Sicilian Mafia to designate a secret thing.

Johnny "Short Fingers" Capaccio and Frank "Greasy Thumb" Guzzo are leading members of la COSA NOSTRA.

> **Nota Bene**
> That the *cosa nostra* exists has been proven repeatedly in court cases and through the testimony of former gangsters. That they ever existed in the romantic form depicted by Mario Puzo in *The Godfather* is another matter entirely. The sordid side of the Mafia lies in their involvement in drugs, prostitution, protection rackets, and so on. The idea that a Mafia don would refuse to involve himself in the drug trade out of moral considerations, as Don Corleone does, beggars the imagination.

C

coup de grâce (French) (koo de GRAHSS) (noun)
A death blow intended to end suffering.

When an execution by firing squad occurs, the person in charge of the firing squad steps forward after the execution and fires a bullet into the head of the victim; this is intended as a kind of symbolic COUP DE GRÂCE.

coup de main (French) (koo de MAHN) (noun)
Literally, "blow of the hand." More generally, a swift, unexpected attack.

Hitler's desperate attempt to win World War II with the Ardennes offensive in the winter of 1944 was a COUP DE MAIN that despite its initial success was doomed to failure because of the Allies' superior resources.

coup de théâtre (French) (koo de tay-A-tre) (noun)
In drama, a sudden, surprising turn of events. Although applied to acting, it can also be practiced in real life.

Convinced that my husband was cheating on me, I decided, in a COUP DE THÉÂTRE, to surprise him at his mistress's house. I didn't realize that the "mistress" was male.

Credo quia absurdum est (Latin) (KRAY-do KWEE-ah ab-SIR-dahm est) (phrase)
I believe because it's absurd. It derives originally from the theologian Tertullian (160–220). Essentially, the phrase captures the idea that religion should be approached as a matter of faith rather than logic.

"Tertullian is credited with the motto CREDO QUIA ABSURDUM—I believe because it is impossible. Needless to say, he began life as a lawyer."
—H. L. Mencken

crème de la crème (French) (KREM de la KREM) (phrase)
Top of the line; best of the best. Based on the fact that cream rises to the top of milk, and so, presumably, the best cream rises to the top of the cream.

Students at Harvard and Yale universities represent the CRÈME DE LA CRÈME of American education—or at least they certainly think they do.

cri du coeur (French) (KREE doo KOOR) (noun)
Literally, "cry from the heart." More generally, any deeply felt exclamation or utterance.

Marcia, in a CRI DU COEUR, exclaimed that she couldn't possibly move from New York City to Omaha because of the lack of good hairdressers.

cui bono (Latin) (koo-ee BO-no) (phrase)
Literally, "to whom is the good." Colloquially, who profits. This is one of the basic questions investigators ask when a crime has been committed.

When we approach the issue of who murdered President John F. Kennedy, we must ask CUI BONO. The answer is clearly the CIA, the Mafia, Cuba, Lyndon Johnson, and the New World Order.

cul-de-sac (French) (KUL de sack) (noun)
Literally, "bottom of the bag." More generally, a dead end. This is particularly used concerning geography, but it can also have broader uses, for instance concerning a line of argument.

The logical contradictions in your position have forced you into a CUL-DE-SAC. Now you've got no choice but to agree with me that the entire universe is the inside of a giant hamster.

cum grano salis (Latin) (koom GRAN-o SAL-iss) (phrase)
With a grain of salt. An expression of skepticism about a statement or belief. The phrase originates with Pliny the Elder (23–79), a natural historian, who recounts an antidote for poison that contained salt. Thus any threat concerning poison should be taken with a grain of salt.

I take stories about the invasion of Roswell, New Mexico, by alien beings CUM GRANO SALIS. Of course, that could explain a lot about New Mexicans.

> **Nota Bene**
> Pliny the Elder's *Naturalis Historia* formed the basis for
> much of early medieval Europe's approach to natural sci-
> ence. Pliny was such a committed scientist that when
> Mount Vesuvius exploded near the ancient town of Pompeii
> in 79, he insisted on going to observe it. Sadly, he perished
> in the attempt; his son Pliny the Younger left an eloquent
> testimony to the courage and intelligence of his father.

C

cum laude (Latin) (koom LOUD-ay) (adv.)
With praise. An academic degree that is taken cum laude indicates a
high level of performance on the part of the degree holder.
> *I don't feel formal education is especially important. It's true I have
> a CUM LAUDE undergraduate degree from Harvard, and a mas-
> ter's and doctorate from Yale, but I hardly ever mention them.*

curriculum vitae (Latin) (kur-IH-cue-lum VEE-tie) (noun)
A summary of one's academic and professional career and achieve-
ments. In academic circles, the equivalent of a resume.
> *We have an open position for professor of philosophy, and Dr. Smith
> of Princeton has been good enough to send me his CURRICULUM
> VITAE, along with the letter of application for the post.*

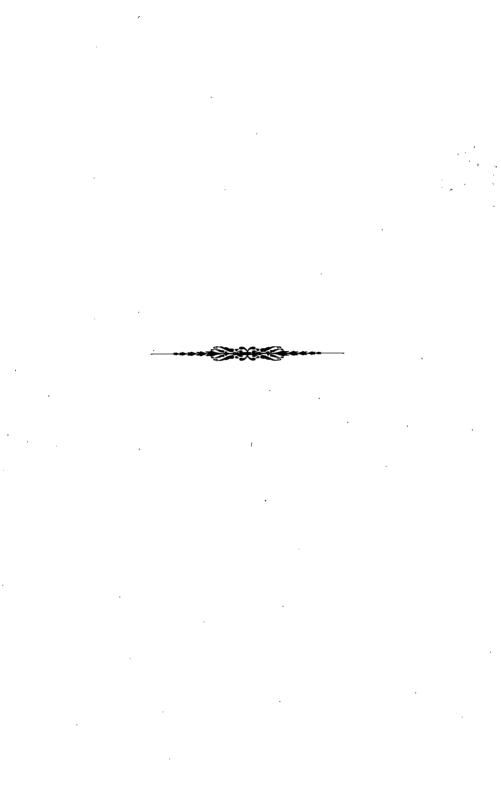

"I just know so many people who have six or seven foreign languages and have read everything and have musical training and they are still dorks."

—Joseph Epstein

D

da capo (Italian) (dah KAHP-oh) (adv.)

Often abbreviated D.C., this is a musical term meaning "from the beginning." When a composer inserts the phrase in a score, it directs the player to return to a designated point in the piece and repeat it.

The score for the overture indicates that the last ten bars are to be played DA CAPO.

D

déclassé (French) (DAY-klass-AY) (adj.)

Lower class; inferior; common. Although the French, in theory, abolished social classes during the French Revolution of 1789, that hasn't stopped them from contributing a number of words that designate social rank and its privileges and penalties.

Please don't wear that plaid shirt to the theater. It's so DÉCLASSÉ— I wouldn't want to be seen anywhere near you.

décolletage (French) (DAY-kole-eh-TAZH) (noun)

The neck and shoulders of a woman that are exposed by a dress, one that particularly emphasizes her cleavage. Again, this is something the French are particularly skilled at: inventing words to describe something sexy. During the eighteenth and nineteenth centuries, French fashions generally indicated that a dress wasn't a dress unless the woman's breasts were half exposed.

That outfit that Jennifer Lopez wore to the Oscars this year particularly emphasized her DÉCOLLETAGE . . . not that that's a bad thing.

de facto (Latin) (dee FAK-toh) (adv.)

In fact; in actuality. Generally, something that occurs in practice even when it is not legally or specifically mandated.

Even though Chicago's schools were supposedly integrated in the 1960s, they remain DE FACTO segregated to a large extent.

De gustibus non est disputandum (Latin) (day GUS-ti-bus non est dis-poo-TAHN-dum) (phrase)

There should be no arguments concerning questions of taste. That is to say, issues of taste are matters of opinion, and so we can't say someone's taste is right or wrong. Although paintings on black velvet of puppies and Elvis push this idea to its limits.

déjà vu (French) (DAY-zha VOO) (noun)
An experience of feeling one has already seen or heard something
before. Émile Boirac (1851–1917), a psychic researcher, first used
this term, and it has since become part of the vernacular.

> *The baseball player Yogi Berra famously remarked of back-to-back*
> *home runs by Mickey Mantel and Roger Maris, "It's DÉJÀ VU all*
> *over again."*

D

Nota Bene
Among the most famous comments of Berra were:

"You've got to be very careful if you don't know where
you're going, because you might not get there."

"Baseball is 90 percent mental—the other half is physical."

"A nickel isn't worth a dime today."

"When you come to a fork in the road, take it."

de jure (Latin) (day ZHU-ray) (adv.)
According to law. The opposite of **de facto.**

> *Unlike in the North, discrimination against African Americans in*
> *the South during the 1950s and 1960s was DE JURE.*

dei gratia (Latin) (DAY-ee GRAH-tee-ah) (adv.)
By the grace of God. Applied particularly to the reign of British mon-
archs. D.G. Regina appears on British coins, indicating "Queen, by
the grace of God." Within the Catholic Church, the phrase is also
applied to upper levels of the ecclesiastical hierarchy.

> *Monsignor Smith has been designated Bishop DEI GRATIA.*

demi-monde (French) (DEH-me -MOND) (noun)
A group of people living a self-indulgent lifestyle. The term has
been particularly applied to sections of the European upper classes
from the late eighteenth to the twentieth centuries. In America,
this group is more commonly referred to as "jet setters," but in any

case the behavior is the same: drinking, gambling, and hanging out at fashionable clubs.

> *Paris Hilton, Kim Kardashian, and Lindsay Lohan are part of the modern American DEMI-MONDE. Evidently standards for this sort of thing have fallen off during the past fifty years.*

De mortuis nil nisi bonum (Latin) (day MOR-too-eess nil niss-ee BON-um) (phrase)
Speak nothing but good of the dead. Refers to the custom that we shouldn't say anything bad about someone who has passed on, a custom honored more in the breach than in the observance.

> *Well, DE MORTUIS NIL NISI BONUM, but I have to say that the late, unlamented Robert Jenkins was a complete son of a bitch.*

de novo (Latin) (day NO-vo) (adv.)
From the beginning; fresh.

> *We intend to approach our relationship DE NOVO, in the hopes of putting all of our backbiting and sniping behind us—to say nothing of my thirteen-year affair with another woman.*

De omnibus dubitandum (Latin) (day AHM-ni-bus DO-bee-than-doom) (phrase)
Be suspicious of everything. The phrase is sometimes attributed to René Descartes (1596–1650), whose philosophy was based on extreme skepticism toward everything (see **Cogito ergo sum**).

> *Given the way that news is often packaged by big corporations these days, DE OMNIBUS DUBITANDUM is probably a good approach when reading the newspaper or watching television.*

deo volente (Latin) (DAY-oh WO-len-tay) (phrase)
God willing. If God allows.

> *This spring, DEO VOLENTE, I'll have a new job and we'll have moved out of our old house. But you never can tell what might happen.*

de profundis (Latin) (day pro-FOON-deess) (phrase)
From the depths. It is the opening of Psalm 130. It is also the title of a book by Oscar Wilde (1854–1900) written during his time in prison after his conviction for sodomy.

After the long, painful struggle of Finals Week, I have arisen DE PROFUNDIS and come forth to the light of day. And to the bar.

> **Nota Bene**
>
> Wilde's book *De Profundis* took the form of a long letter to his former lover, Lord Alfred Douglas. Douglas's father, the Marquess of Queensberry, had left an insulting note for Wilde at his club, publicly accusing the poet of sodomy. Wilde, against the advice of his friends and at the urging of Douglas, sued the Marquess. As a result of the revelations produced at the trial, Wilde was charged with sodomy, convicted, and sentenced to two years in prison. He died shortly after his release.

D

de rien (French) (deh REE-en) (phrase)
It's nothing. Nothing important.
    What's that I said? DE RIEN. Nothing of any importance.

de rigueur (French) (deh ree-GERR) (adv.)
Required; mandated. Often used concerning fashion, but it can be applied to just about anything.
    This year, the fashionistas have declared that black leather boots are DE RIGEUR for casual wear.

dernier cri (French) (DARE-nee-air KREE) (adj.)
Literally, "the last cry." Colloquially, the latest fashion.
    I remember when Jungian literary criticism was the DERNIER CRI in English departments around the country.

derrière (French) (DEH-ree-AIR) (noun)
Bottom; butt. A French (therefore, much sexier) way to refer to someone's ass.
    Jennifer Lopez says that her best feature is her DERRIÈRE. She claims she stares at it in the mirror for hours.

desaparecidos (Spanish) (dess-AH-par-ay-SEE-doss) (noun)
People who have disappeared. In Latin America, this has come to refer to those people abducted and murdered either by the government or by rival political factions.

> *During the authoritarian rule of Augusto Pinochet in Chile, tens of thousands of DESAPARECIDOS were reported by human rights groups; most of their bodies were never found.*

de trop (French) (deh TROH) (adj.)
Too much; excessive.

> *The exterior detailing on that building is really DE TROP. It detracts from the architect's overall statement.*

dolce far niente (Italian) (DOL-chay fahr NEE-en-tay) (noun)
Literally, "sweet doing nothing." More generally, a happy or delicious idleness. Blissful relaxation, of the kind that is accentuated by watching someone else at work while you remain idle.

> *We spent an afternoon at the beach, dozing in the sun, enjoying the DOLCE FAR NIENTE of summer vacation.*

dolce vita (Italian) (DOHL-chay VEE-ta) (noun)
The sweet life. A lifestyle in which the mind and the senses are gratified.

> *We're here in the Greek Islands, living la DOLCE VITA, eating grapes and cheese and sipping wine while looking at the blue waters of the Mediterranean that surround us. Wish you were here.*

deus ex machina (Latin) (DAY-us ex MAH-kee-nah) (noun)
A dramatic or literary device that steps in from the outside to resolve plot problems. Generally, this is disliked by writers, but that doesn't stop many of them from using it in their works.

> *Charles Dickens was a devotee of the DEUS EX MACHINA, the "good rich man" who steps in at the last moment to resolve all of the hero's issues and impose a happy ending.*

D

> **Nota Bene**
> Although the term *deus ex machina* is Latin, the original
> concept was Greek. The Latin literally means "god out of
> the machine" and refers to the sudden appearance in Greek
> plays of gods who descended from above, lowered onto the
> stage by a kind of hook or crane. Aristotle, in his *Poetics*,
> objected strongly to this sort of plot device.

deus vult (Latin) (DAY-us WULT) (interjection)
God wills it! When Pope Urban II preached the First Crusade in
1095, his listeners were said to be so moved at the prospect of
regaining the Holy Land that they rose and with one voice shouted,
"Deus Vult." Soldiers from across Western Europe began to sew
crosses on their clothing and declare their intention of taking up
arms in the name of Christ to seize the holy city of Jerusalem.
Suffice it to say, this didn't end well.

dharma (Sanskrit) (DAR-mah) (noun)
Natural law, or the natural order of things. To follow one's dharma
is to align oneself with the working out of the natural universe,
something that is the aspiration of Buddhists, Hindus, and other
practitioners of Eastern religions.
> *I believe my DHARMA is to be a fast-food restaurant worker, so that's
> why I haven't tried to get another job. Of course, I could be wrong.*

**Die ganzen Zahlen hat der liebe Gott gemacht, alles andere
ist Menschenwerk** (German) (DEE GAHN-zen ZAH-len hat der
LEEB-eh got ge-MACHT al-lez AN-dar-reh ist MENSH-en-verk)
(quotation)
Dear God made whole numbers; the rest is man's work.
—Leopold Kronecker (1823–1891)

dies irae (Latin) (DEE-ase EE-rye) (noun)
The Day of Wrath; another term for Judgment Day. In the Middle
Ages, Thomas of Celano (1200–c.1265) wrote a poem with this title
that was eventually turned into a hymn that became part of the
Roman Catholic Mass.

dieu et mon droit (French) (DEE-oo ay mon DRWAH) (phrase)
God and my right. The motto of the monarchy of England. And lest you think it a tad weird that the British monarchy's motto should be in French, remember that in the fifteenth century when this motto was first adopted, substantial parts of what we now think of as France were under the control of the British crown. Not that this stopped the British and French from hating each other's guts—it just made the conflict a little more intimate.

divide et impera (Latin) (dee-VEE-day et IM-pair-ah) (phrase)
Divide and conquer. A political strategy that actually goes back a long way before the time of the Romans, who thought up this slogan, and has lasted up to the present day.
In a strategy of DIVIDE ET IMPERA, the United States supported various Iraqi factions against one another in that country's civil war.

docendo discitur (Latin) (do-KEN-do DIS-kit-ur) (phrase)
Something is learned by teaching. A comment by the Roman Stoic Seneca (4 B.C.– A.D. 65). More generally, the best way to learn something is to teach it to someone else.
I discovered that DOCENDO DISCITUR, I understand math much better since having to tutor my little brother in his algebra class.

dominus vobiscum (Latin) (DOM-i-nus wo-BISS-kum) (interjection)
The Lord be with you. Traditionally, this is used in the Roman Catholic Mass. The correct response is et cum spirito tuo (and with your spirit).

dona nobis pacem (Latin) (DO-nah NO-biss PAH-kem) (phrase)
Give us peace. This is a traditional Christian hymn as well as the theme of a number of musical works, including J. S. Bach's *Mass in B Minor* and "Pray Your Gods" by Toad the Wet Sprocket.

Doppelgänger (German) (DOP-el-GANG-er) (noun)
Literally, a "double walker." Someone who is the precise duplicate of someone else. Unlike twins, doppelgängers need not be related,

and in fact generally aren't. They are usually a portent of evil. In general usage, the word can also refer to an object or an idea.

When we were out walking the other day, I saw someone who was my Uncle Ralph's DOPPLEGÄNGER. I had to call him to make sure he was still in Buffalo and not New Jersey.

D

dramatis personae (Latin) (drah-MA-tiss pair-SONE-eye) (noun)
In theater, a list of the actors and their roles in a play. It is occasionally used to refer to the people involved in a particular event.

In the election controversy of 2000, DRAMATIS PERSONAE included Al Gore, George W. Bush, and Florida Secretary of State Katherine Harris, as well as, eventually, members of the Supreme Court.

dreck (Yiddish) (DREK) (noun)
Nonsense; trash.

Supermarket tabloids publish the most awful DRECK about celebrities. Almost none of it's true, but we keep buying them anyway. After all, who doesn't want to know the details of Kim Kardashian's divorce?

du jour (French) (doo ZHOOR) (adv.)
Of the day; current. French menus refer to plats du jour, chef's daily specials.

Rather than embrace the academic philosophy DU JOUR, I prefer to spend time refining my world view into one I can stick with and defend.

Dulce et decorum est pro patria mori (Latin) (DUL-kay et day-COR-oom est pro PAT-ree-ah MOR-ee) (quotation)
How sweet and worthy it is to die for one's country. This line from Horace (65 B.C.–8 B.C.) was originally intended seriously (expressing a general Roman view of patriotism). During World War I it was used by the antiwar poet Wilfred Owen (1893–1918) as the title of a poem to express disillusionment with patriotism and attack those who asked young men to die for the glory of their country. Ironically, Owen himself was killed in the closing weeks of the war.

dum spiro spero (Latin) (doom SPEE-roh SPAY-roh) (phrase)
While I breathe, I hope. Or, while there's life, there's hope.

> *I may have failed every exam this semester and not turned in any of my papers to my professor, but I'm optimistic I'll pull through this class somehow. DUM SPIRO SPERO!*

Dummkopf (German) (DOOM-kopf) (noun)
Literally, "stupid head." Dummy; idiot.

> *Watch where you're driving, DUMMKOPF! Can't you see I've got the right of way?*

Dura lex sed lex (Latin) (DOO-rah lex said lex) (phrase)
The law is hard, but it's the law. Alternately, deal with it! A phrase that should be of considerable use to parents everywhere.

> *Your curfew is 10 P.M., and I don't care how late you want to stay out with your friends. DURA LEX SED LEX!*

"Parents should conduct their arguments in quiet, respectful tones, but in a foreign language. You'd be surprised what an inducement that is to the education of children."

—Judith Martin

E

Ecce homo (Latin) (EK-ay HO-mo) (interjection)
According to Christian doctrine, this is what Pontius Pilate said when Jesus of Nazareth was brought before him for judgment. The original of the quotation is from the King James Bible, a translation of the Greek Septuagint. At various points it has been the title of paintings illustrating the life and passion of Christ.

ego te absolvo (Latin) (ay-go tay ab-SOLV-oh) (phrase)
I absolve you. Part of the Sacrament of Penance in the Catholic Church: *Deinde, ego te absolvo a peccatis tuis in nomina Patris, et Filii, et Spiritus Sancti.* (Thus I absolve you of your sins in the name of the Father, and of the Son, and of the Holy Ghost.) Performance of this sacrament removed the possibility of Hell if the sinner is truly repentant.

élan (French) (AY-lahn) (noun)
Ardor or enthusiasm.
> *She showed great energy and ÉLAN on the ski slope, outdistancing her compatriots by a wide margin.*

embonpoint (French) (em-bon-PWAHNT) (noun)
Stoutness; a tendency toward plumpness or roundness. Chubby.
> *He displayed the EMBONPOINT characteristic of those accustomed to linger over their meals for three or four hours.*

emeritus (Latin) (ay-MARE-i-tus) (adj.)
Designating someone who has retired at a particular rank. It is particularly applied to figures in the military, the Church, or academia.
> *Professor Smith, upon his retirement, assumed the position of Professor EMERITUS of American History, in which capacity he taught one class every semester—the same number of classes he had taught before stepping down.*

éminence grise (French) (Eh-may-nonss GREEZ) (noun)
Literally, "a gray eminence." A respected elder figure who is an expert in a particular field.
> *Dr. Henry Kissinger is an ÉMINENCE GRISE of American diplomacy, despite being considered a war criminal in a number of countries around the world.*

en famille (French) (AHN fah-MEE) (adj.)
In the bosom of your family; surrounded by family members.
I intend to spend this holiday season EN FAMILLE, which should have both positive and negative aspects. If we survive it, I'm sure we'll all have a merry Christmas.

enfant terrible (French) (AHN-fahnt tare-EE-bl) (noun)
Literally, "terrible infant." Colloquially, a preternaturally precocious or gifted child or one who in some other way presents a unique challenge to his parents and caregivers. It has also come to mean anyone young who shows signs of rebellion.
Elected to the Senate at the age of thirty-five, Senator Jones quickly became the ENFANT TERRIBLE of Capitol Hill, proposing more than two dozen bills in his first two years in office.

en garde (French) (ahn GAHRD) (interjection)
On guard! A warning at the beginning of a fencing match that signals the start of the match. More generally, a warning that a conflict is about to begin.
You have challenged me to a dominoes tournament. Be aware that I have been the Passaic, New Jersey, dominoes champion for three years running. EN GARDE!

en masse (French) (ahn-MASS) (adv.)
In its entirety. As a group. Referring to an action taken by a large group of people.
The drama critics descended EN MASSE upon Spider-Man: Turn Off the Dark *and, quite rightfully, tore it to shreds.*

ennui (French) (ahn-WE) (noun)
Boredom. Tedium.
The pages of the London Review of Books *post-1973 elicit from one an ineluctable ENNUI, from which it is almost impossible to recover.*

en passant (French) (ahn pass-AHNT) (adv.)
Literally, "in passing." A move in chess in which a pawn moves forward two spaces and an opposing pawn captures it on the next move as if it had moved only one space. The term arises from the

fact that the first pawn is prevented from simply passing the opposing pawn without the possibility of capture.

> **Nota Bene**
> Among the earliest chess experts was the Spanish player Ruy López (1530–1580). One of the most popular openings in chess is named for him because it was included in his book *Libro de la invencion liberal y arte del juego del axedrez*. In fact, this is the first chess opening to be recorded, and thus, one of the most systematically studied.

en plein air (French) (ahn PLEHN air) (adj.)
In the open air. Particularly referring to the practice of painting outside. This was particularly practiced in the nineteenth century, both in Europe and in America. In the United States, a school sprang up based on painting in the open air located in the Hamptons in Long Island, New York. French impressionists were strongly influenced by plein air painting techniques as well.
   Many of Vincent Van Gogh's most famous paintings, such as his depictions of the countryside of Arles, were painted EN PLEIN AIR.

en rapport (French) (ahn rah-PORR) (adv.)
In sympathy; in accordance with.
   My boyfriend and I discovered we were both EN RAPPORT in regard to both politics and Arrested Development.

entente cordiale (French) (ah-TANT cor-dyAHL) (noun)
A favorable alliance; a happy relationship between two countries or states—or, occasionally, people. Specifically, this refers to a series of agreements signed between Britain and France prior to the First World War. Although the two countries had been at almost continuous war since the beginning of the Middle Ages, they managed to bury their differences long enough to agree that they hated Germany and the Austro-Hungarian empire more than each other. This pleasant situation endured until approximately ten minutes after peace was declared in 1918.

Although Jennifer and I have fought over everything, from the wedding china to the division of pets in the divorce, we did manage, at last, to achieve an ENTENTE CORDIALE on the subject of her mother.

E

entre nous (French) (AHN-treh NOO) (adv.)
Between us; between ourselves.
ENTRE NOUS, I can't imagine that this new reconciliation between George and Jennifer is going to last. But you know them better than I.

Epistula non erubescit (Latin) (ay-PISS-too-lah non air-OOB-eh-SKIT) (quotation)
"A letter doesn't blush." .
—Cicero (106 B.C.–43 B.C.)

e pluribus unum (Latin) (AY PLOO-ree-bus OO-num) (motto)
From many, one. The motto found on the Great Seal of the United States, as well as on its currency. In 1956 Congress made the official motto of the country "In God we trust"; until that time *e pluribus unum* had been considered the country's unofficial motto.

ergo (Latin) (AIR-go) (conj.)
Therefore.
I am a brilliant thinker, ERGO no one understands me. Isn't it always the way?

Errare humanum est (Latin) (air-ARE-ay hoo-MAHN-oom est) (phrase)
To err is human. Originally from St. Augustine of Hippo (354–430). Often quoted as "To err is human, to forgive, divine."
Before you accuse me of having an extramarital affair, I think you should remember that ERRARE HUMANUM EST.

ersatz (German) (air-SATZ) (adj.)
Substitute; replacement. Typically used of something inferior; it was particularly applied during the Second World War to replacements for staples that were in short supply.

During the war, we had to make do with ERSATZ coffee brewed from chicory or other, less palatable alternatives.

esprit de corps (French) (ehs-PREE de COR) (noun)
Team spirit; camaraderie.
> *The fact that our football team lost sixty-four games in a row gave us, oddly, a certain ESPRIT DE CORPS. We were united by our inferiority.*

et alii (Latin) (et AL-ee-ee) (noun)
And others. Normally abbreviated "et al."
> *This book was written by Robert D. Smith, Elaine Smith, ET ALII.*

et cetera (Latin) (et SET-er-ah) (adv.)
And the rest; and so on. Normally abbreviated etc.
> *The room is filled with poets, writers, artists, ET CETERA.*

Et in Arcadia ego (Latin) (et in ar-KAH-dee-ah AY-go) (phrase)
And I, too, have lived in Arcadia.More generally, I too, have enjoyed the pleasures of this world (implying that I do so no longer). Arcadia was an area of the Greek Peloponnesus that was inhabited primarily by shepherds; thus the term "Arcadia" came, in Classical literature, to refer to a pastoral life. This sort of life was regarded as ideal by many Classical authors, something to be aspired to.
> *Although I'm now an elder and highly respected member of the Conservative community, ET IN ARCADIA EGO. When I was young, I attended rock concerts by cutting-edge bands like Abba.*

Nota Bene

The Roman poet Virgil (70 B.C.–19 B.C.) in his *Eclogues* espoused the joys of the pastoral life. Many centuries later, the French painter Nicholas Poussin (1594–1665) used the expression "Et in Arcadia ego" as the title of a painting depicting Greek shepherds gathered around an ancient tomb bearing this inscription. The phrase also appears in a somewhat different context as the title of the first part of Evelyn Waugh's (1903–1966) novel, *Brideshead Revisited.*

Et tu, Brute? (Latin) (et TOO broo-TAY) (phrase)
Even you, Brutus? The words supposedly spoken by Julius Caesar (100 B.C.–44 B.C.) upon his assassination on March 15, 44 B.C. Among those taking part in his murder was his former friend Marcus Junius Brutus (85 B.C.–42 B.C.), and Caesar, in his dying breath, reproved him for his betrayal. (The legend of this reproach is probably apocryphal.) Thus, this exclamation has come to be applied to any act of treachery, particularly one committed by a close friend.

> *Someone told me that even though you and I spent all last year hanging out together, at a party the other night you were making fun of me. ET TU, BRUTE?*

eureka (Greek) (you-REE-kah) (interjection)
I have found it. According to legend, this was the word shouted by the great Greek inventor and mathematician Archimedes of Syracuse (287 B.C.–212 B.C.) when, while sitting in his bath, he conceived of the principle of displacement. According to some accounts, he ran naked down the street, shouting to his neighbors, who, quite possibly, were used to that sort of thing from him.

> *EUREKA! I've finally discovered the proportions needed to mix the perfect gin and tonic.*

ex animo (Latin) (eks AN-i-mo) (adv.)
From the heart; from the soul. Thus, sincerely.

> *Please believe me that my declaration of everlasting love and devotion is EX ANIMO.*

ex cathedra (Latin) (eks kah-THAY-drah) (adv.)
From a seat of authority. Applied particularly to the Catholic Church, to those pronouncements that come from the pope concerning matters of doctrine. In these matters, since 1870 the pope has been deemed infallible.

> *The Catholic Church has reaffirmed its opposition to abortion and many forms of birth control in a series of EX CATHEDRA statements.*

excelsior (Latin) (eks-SELL-see-or) (adv.)
Literally, "higher." Its most famous use is in a (bad) poem by Henry
Wadsworth Longfellow, which begins
>*The shades of night were falling fast,*
>*As through an Alpine village passed*
>*A youth, who bore mid snow and ice,*
>*A banner with the strange device,*
>*Excelsior!*

And so on. You get the general idea.

excusez-moi (French) (eks-SKOOZ-ay MWAH) (interjection)
Excuse me.
>*EXCUSEZ-MOI. I didn't mean to bump your arm back there and
>make you drop that entire tray of crystal wine glasses.*

exempli gratia (Latin) (eks-EMP-lee GRAH-tee-ah) (prepositional
phrase)
For the sake of example; for instance.
>*In discussing the awful state of American culture today, let's con-
>sider, EXEMPLI GRATIA, the unwarranted attention paid to Kim
>Kardashian's seventy-two-day "marriage."*

ex gratia (Latin) (eks GRAH-tee-ah) (adv.)
By favor; that is, from kindness or generosity rather than because
of compulsion.
>*Because he has said that billionaires should pay more taxes, many
>people have urged Warren Buffet to make an EX GRATIA payment
>to the U.S. Treasury.*

ex libris (Latin) (eks LEE-briss) (adv.)
From the library. This is a common phrase found on book plates
(well, it would be a common phrase if anyone used book plates anymore) and is followed by the owner's name.
>*EX LIBRIS Peter Archer (not to be removed by anyone else).*

Ex nihilo nihil fit (Latin) (eks NIL-oh NE-hil FIT) (phrase)
Nothing comes from nothing. This is a very ancient argument used
by Greek philosophers (particularly Aristotle) to justify the idea of
a First Cause. The world, they argued, must have existed in some

form from eternity, since to say otherwise was to believe that matter could be created from nothing. The idea was expressed in this form by Empedocles (490 B.C.–430 B.C.)

ex officio (Latin) (eks oh-FIK-ee-oh) (adv.)
Literally "from office." More generally, this refers to someone who holds one position by virtue of holding another.

The president of the United States is EX OFFICIO the commander in chief of American armed forces.

ex parte (Latin) (eks PAHR-tay) (adv.)
From one person or party. A legal decision occasionally doesn't require that both parties to the dispute be present; such a decision is referred to as "ex parte."

Since my spouse disappeared, taking all of our money with him, the judge rendered an EX PARTE decision granting me a divorce.

ex post facto (Latin) (eks post FAK-toh) (phrase)
Literally, "from after the fact." Retrospectively. A law or a decision that is implemented "ex post facto" is one that affects issues or circumstances that existed prior to the law or decision's enactment.

The decision by some states EX POST FACTO to rewrite their death penalty laws has meant that many prisoners have been removed from death row.

"Never knew before what eternity was made for. It is to give some of us a chance to learn German."

—Mark Twain

F

façade (French) (fah-SAHD) (noun)
Literally, "face." One exterior side of a building, usually intended to be seen by the largest number of people and thus more elaborately decorated than the other sides. From this, the word has come to imply an insincere appearance.

> *Although Robert is a highly unpleasant person, in order to keep his job he has to preserve a FAÇADE of civility.*

facsimile (Latin) (FAK-si-mi-LEE) (noun)
Made alike. Thus, the modern usage of the word, reproduction. Ideally, a facsimile should be as accurate a copy of the original as possible, including any flaws and imperfections that might occur.

> *In my living room, you'll find a FACSIMILE of Da Vinci's St. Anne with Virgin and Child, which proves I'm very sophisticated, since a less knowledgeable person would have had a copy of the Mona Lisa.*

facta non verba (Latin) (FAK-tah non WERB-ah) (phrase)
Deeds, not words. Colloquially, don't say it, do it.

> *I'm sick and tired of everyone chattering on about the weather. FACTA NON VERBA! It's time we did something about it!*

fait accompli (French) (FEHT a-kohm-PLEE) (noun)
An accomplished deed. Usually refers to something that has been done before anyone is fully aware of it or, possibly, has approved of it.

> *I'm afraid the secret documents have already been published on Wikileaks, so it's a bit of a FAIT ACCOMPLI.*

faute de mieux (French) (FOHT de MYUH) (phrase)
For want of anything better. For lack of a superior plan.

> *I realize that going to see the latest Sandra Bullock movie may not be to everyone's taste, but FAUTE DE MIEUX, I think we're stuck with it.*

faux pas (French) (foh PAH) (noun)
Error; mistake. Usually one that is tasteless and embarrassing by its obviousness.

> *Wearing shorts and a tee shirt to my grandfather's funeral was a serious FAUX PAS, according to my grandmother.*

Feinschmecker (German) (FINE-shmek-er) (noun)
Gourmet. One who appreciates food.
> *As one who dines only in four-star restaurants, I have a well-earned reputation as a FEINSCHMECKER to rival that of Anthony Bourdain.*

femme fatale (French) (FEM fah-TAHL) (noun)
Literally, "deadly woman." A dangerous or treacherous woman who is also beautiful and seductive. In fact, she uses her charms to ensnare the unwary.
> *In my dreams, I'm often entangled with a FEMME FATALE like Mata Hari or Barbara Stanwyck. Or sometimes Jessica Rabbit.*

.F

Nota Bene
Among the earliest filmic examples of a femme fatale was Theda Bara (1885–1955). She originated the term "vamp" and was the object of men's desires everywhere. Her name was an anagram for "Arab Death," and she was notorious for wearing (for the period) revealing costumes and slithering across the screen to seduce foolish men. Sadly, few of her films have been preserved, although today's "sex symbols" like Paris Hilton could learn a lot from her.

festina lente (Latin) (FESS-tee-nah LEN-tay) (phrase)
Make haste slowly. More broadly, if you rush a job, it will take you longer, whereas if you take the time to get it right, it will be done sooner. In other words, Haste makes waste.
> *Just remember when you're cleaning my Porsche, FESTINA LENTE. Take your time. This car should be treated with proper reverence.*

Festschrift (German) (FEST-shrift) (noun)
A collection of academic essays in honor of a professor. The collection, which is normally themed around the professor's area of specialization, is often assembled late in the scholar's career when she or he is on the verge of retiring. Thus it is more or less academia's equivalent of the traditional gold watch.

Hogwarts faculty is proud to present this FESTSCHRIFT to Professor McGonagall, essays dealing with the problems of transfiguration.

Fiat justitia ruat caelum (Latin) (FEE-aht joo-STEE-see-ah ROO-at KI-lum) (phrase)
Let justice be done, though the heavens fall. The origins of the phrase are uncertain; it is associated, perhaps wrongly, with Lucius Calpurnius Piso (d. 43 B.C.). It is generally taken to mean that justice should be carried out and let the chips fall where they may.

fiat lux (Latin) (FEE-aht LUX) (phrase)
Let there be light. The Latin translation of a phrase occurring in Genesis: And God said, Let there be light: and there was light. The phrase is the motto of a number of institutions, including such diverse organizations as the University of Akron, Queen's College in Barbados, and St. Andrew's School in Bloemfontein, South Africa.

fides quaerens intellectum (Latin) (FEE-dayz KWI-rens in-tell-EK-toom) (phrase)
Faith seeking understanding. A phrase associated with St. Anselm (1033–1109), a leading theologian of the early Middle Ages. There has been much argument among scholars about what exactly Anselm was getting at, but the general consensus these days seems to be that Anselm believed that one's love of God (faith) should drive one toward a deeper knowledge of God (understanding).

film noir (French) (film NWAHR) (noun)
A kind of filmmaking popularized in the 1930s and 1940s in Europe and America. A film noir is generally a mystery or thriller, often one in which the theme of moral ambiguity plays a central role. Thus the detective is often as unscrupulous as the villains. Women are often beautiful and treacherous (see **femme fatale**).

> **Nota Bene**
> Among the most important examples of film noir are *The Maltese Falcon* (1941) directed by John Huston; *The Postman Always Rings Twice* (1946) directed by Tay Garnett; and more recently, *Chinatown* (1974) directed by Roman Polanski.

fin de siècle (French) FAN de see-EK-le) (phrase)
End of the century. It's most often used to refer to the period of 1895–1910, a period when European culture, in particular, underwent a substantial transformation with the onset of modernism. At the same time, it suggests that at the end of the nineteenth century, the energy and innovation of the Victorian era was played out. Thus, the term can also refer to a kind of cultural degeneration.

> *The Post impressionists are so FIN DE SIÈCLE; one can see them shrugging off the restraining conventions of their age and anticipating the twentieth century's preoccupation with pure Art.*

flagrante delicto (Latin) (flah-GRAHN-tay day-LIK-to) (phrase)
Literally, "blazing offense." More generally, caught red-handed or in the middle of actually doing something illegal. It's often applied to someone caught in the middle of the sex act.

> *After the wedding, I surprised one of the bridesmaids with the best man in FLAGRANTE DELICTO behind the altar.*

flâneur (French) (fla-NOOR) (noun)
From the French for "stroller" or "lounger," it refers to a person of leisure who strolls about the city, usually well dressed and well spoken. This definition is largely the work of the poet Charles Baudelaire (1821–1867). It has also come to have the meaning of one who "strolls" intellectually as well as physically.

> *In my exploration of the writings of nineteenth-century poets, I have become something of a FLÂNEUR, strolling through the avenues of their minds and souls.*

folie à deux (French) (FOH-lee ah DUH) (phrase)
In a clinical sense, a madness or delusional belief shared by two people. In a somewhat nicer context, it can be used to suggest two people sharing a common intense interest in something.

> *Let us, my love, share a FOLIE À DEUX and wander the streets in the rain until our clothes are soaked through and we can return and sit in a warm bath, sipping champagne.*

fons et origo (Latin) (FONZ et OR-ee-go) (phrase)
Literally, "the font and origin." The originating point of something.
He regards himself as the FONS ET ORIGO of all information about Shakespeare, even though he's never actually seen any of the plays performed.

force majeure (French) (FORSS mah-ZHOOR) (noun)
Superior force, referring to something that is an unavoidable accident. In legal contracts, especially those having to do with insurance, it refers to an occurrence that couldn't have been anticipated by the signers of the contract.
For the purposes of this contract, an alien invasion shall be regarded as a FORCE MAJEURE and in no way affect the rest of the terms of the agreement.

Fortes fortuna adiuvat (Latin) (FOR-tayz for-TOO-nah add-you-WHAT) (phrase)
Fortune favors the bold. Originally used by the playwright Terence (c. 190 B.C.–159 B.C.); it also occurs at the end of Virgil's poem *The Aeneid*.
To your complaint that we're taking too great a risk with this merger, I can only reply FORTES FORTUNA ADIUVAT. If we're willing to be bold, we'll reap great rewards.

"It's important to me to work in my own language now and then. I love English, but you can never learn to master a foreign language if you're not brought up with it."

—Max von Sydow

Gaudeamus igitur (Latin) (gow-day-AH-mus IG-i-tur) (phrase)
Let us, therefore, rejoice. This is the title of a popular university song in many European countries, telling students to remember that life is short and they should enjoy it. One verse (to give you an idea of the tone of the song) runs:

Long live all girls,
Easy and beautiful
Long live older ones too
Tender, lovable,
Good and hardworking.

G

Gemeinschaft (German) (ge-MINE-shaft) (noun)
Community. A concept developed by German sociologists in the late nineteenth century to contrast various types of associations. See **Gesellschaft**.

In a GEMEINSCHAFT, individuals pay attention to the interests of the community as well as to their own; for instance, this is the way a family works.

Gemütlichkeit (German) (ge-MUT-lik-kite) (noun)
Somewhere that is cozy and comfortable; a sense of belonging.

In our little group of friends, I find GEMÜTLICHKEIT cemented by our common experiences and plenty of drinking.

genius loci (Latin) (JEE-nee-us LO-kee) (noun)
Originally this referred to a god or gods who protected a place. However, in more recent usage it has come to mean the spirit or atmosphere of a place.

I've spent many hours in Florida attempting to imbibe its GENIUS LOCI, but still I can't imagine why anyone wants to live there.

Gesamtkunstwerk (German) (geh-ZAHMT-kunst-VERK) (noun)
A total work of art. The term was popularized by the German composer Richard Wagner (1813–1883) to summarize his notion that in opera, the music, scenery, acting, and singing should all be integrated into a harmonious whole.

G

Gesellschaft (German) (ge-ZELL-shaft) (noun)
In contrast to **Gemeinschaft** (see previous), Gesellschaft was seen by the nineteenth-century German sociologists who came up with this idea as equivalent to society, one in which individuals pursue their own interests without necessarily focusing on the good of the whole.

The Tea Party movement conceives of the United States as a GESELLSCHAFT, in which everyone does her or his own thing without interference by or concern for others.

Gestalt (German) (geh-SHTAHLT) (noun/adv.)
Literally "form" or "shape." It is the basis of Gestalt psychology, which argues that the brain is a holistic entity with self-organizing tendencies. In general, this school believes that the brain has an innate organizational form, rather than one imposed on it from outside stimuli.

gesundheit (German) (geh-ZUND-hite) (interjection)
What you say to someone who's sneezed. The word's origins are confusing; *gesund* means "healthy." It's speculated by some linguists that the term originated in the Middle Ages as a blessing against the bubonic plague—although you probably shouldn't mention that the next time someone has to blow their nose in your presence.

glasnost (Russian) (GLAHZ-nost) (noun)
Literally, "openness." Generally, this refers to the policies implemented by Mikhail Gorbachev (1931–) as leader of the Communist Party of the Soviet Union. These policies eventually led to the disintegration of Communism in the USSR and eventually to the end of the Soviet state. Gorbachev's original intention in using the

word seems to have been to reduce corruption in the party and the bureaucracy, but the movement quickly spread beyond its original boundaries.

> *In the wake of recent corporate scandals, I think our company has to rebuild customer trust by pursuing a policy of GLASNOST—starting with releasing the names of our executives and their salaries.*

Gloria in excelsis Deo (Latin) (GLO-ree-ah in eks-CHEL-seess DAY-oh) (phrase)
Glory to God in the highest. This is the beginning of a well-known hymn, echoing the words of the angels to shepherds as they announced the birth of Jesus. The Latin translation was made by Hilary of Poitiers (c. 300–368).

gonif (Yiddish) (GAH-niff) (noun)
A thief; a dishonest person.

> *That Bernie Madoff was a GONIF who should be kept in jail forever for all the money he stole from people.*

Götterdämmerung (German) (gah-ter-DAM-er-ung) (noun)
Twilight of the gods. Also the name of a well-known opera by Wagner (see **Gesamtkunstwerke**). The original Norse legend on which Wagner drew for his story predicted that a war among the gods would lead to the end of the world. Thus the word today is sometimes used to mean a period of catastrophic decline or apocalypse.

> *During 2008, it seemed as if we were seeing GÖTTERDÄMMER-UNG enacted on Wall Street, as financial houses collapsed.*

Nota Bene
Adolf Hitler (1889–1945) was a great devotee of Wagner, as were many in his inner circle of advisers. As Berlin trembled before the advance of Soviet armies in April 1945, it was therefore ironic that the final piece played by the Berlin Philharmonic was the final scene from *Götterdämmerung*.

Gott ist tot! (German) (GOT ist TOTE) (phrase)
God is dead. Friedrich Nietzsche (1844–1900), the German philosopher, put forward this proposition in *The Gay Science*, first pub-

lished in 1882, and in *Thus Spoke Zarathustra* between 1883 and 1885. He meant that in particular the Christian concept of God no longer had any relevance to modern society. However, his meaning became vulgarized by later commentators, who assumed Nietzsche was proclaiming himself an atheist.

G

Gott würfelt nicht (German) (GOT ver-FELT NIKT) (phrase)
God does not play dice. This comment, made by physicist Albert Einstein (1879–1955), expressed the feeling of many physicists of the mid–twentieth century that something must be radically wrong with the theory of quantum mechanics, since it implied that there were certain elements of nature that were inherently uncertain or unknowable. Einstein preferred to pursue his unified field theory, in an effort to find a universal theory of physics.

goy (Yiddish) (goy) (noun)
Non-Jew. It is derived from the Hebrew term for "nation."
I hear Miriam brought home a GOY as her boyfriend rather than a nice Jewish boy.

grande dame (French) (grahnd dame) (noun)
A great lady. A woman who is highly respected. Although the term has tended to be applied to society women, more recently it's been used to describe eminent women from all walks of life, especially those with high public profiles.
Hillary Clinton is now seen as the GRANDE DAME of American politics.

Grand Guignol (French) (GRAHN geen-YOLE) (noun)
Originally a theater in Montmartre, an area of Paris. During its existence from 1897 to 1962, it offered shows of often grotesque spectacles, including abundant use of stage blood and other devices meant to horrify as well as entertain the audience. Thus the term has come to mean any outsized and weird spectacle.
Splatter horror films, with their explicit violence, have become the GRANDE GUIGNOL of modern American cinema.

graviora manent (Latin) (grah-we-OR-ah MAN-ent) (phrase)
Greater troubles remain. The worse is yet to come.
> *You may think we've gotten through winter because it's the end of February, but trust me, GRAVIORA MANENT.*

G

gringo (Spanish) (GREEN-go) (noun)
Slang for non-Hispanic person; Caucasian. The word dates back to the eighteenth century but only came into common use in the twentieth century with the spread of Spanish in the United States.
> *Isn't it a little weird that most of the people who like Tex-Mex food are GRINGOS?*

gulag (Russian) (GOO-lahg) (noun)
An acronym for Chief Administration of Corrective Labor Camps and Colonies, this word quickly came to mean both the general system of labor camps set up in the Soviet Union and, more generally, any widely repressive prison system. Although the gulag was formally dissolved in 1960, the system of camps persisted until the end of the Soviet Union.

> **Nota Bene**
> The Soviet gulag inspired a considerable amount of literature, most notably Alexandr Solzhenitsyn's (1918–2008) *One Day in the Life of Ivan Denisovich* and *The Gulag Archipelago*. As well, Nadezha Mandelstam (1899–1980), in her books *Hope Against Hope* and *Hope Abandoned*, recounts her life and that of her husband, Osip, in the gulag.

"I have never known what is Arabic or English, or which one was really mine beyond any doubt. What I do know, however, is that the two have always been together in my life, one resonating in the other, sometimes ironically, sometimes nostalgically, most often each correcting, and commenting on, the other. Each can seem like my absolutely first language, but neither is."

—Edward Said

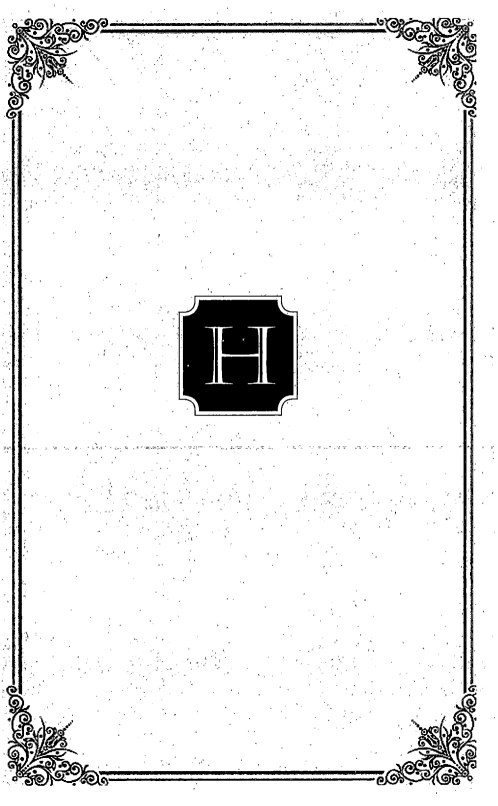

habeas corpus (Latin) (HAY-be-us COR-puss) (noun)
Literally, "You may have the body." The legal action by which someone is released from custody if a judge decides there is not enough evidence to hold her or him.

> *Although it was severely damaged by the Patriot Act in the wake of the September 11, 2001, attacks, the principle of HABEAS CORPUS is generally upheld in the United States.*

haiku (Japanese) (hi-KOO) (noun)
A Japanese poetic form, consisting of seventeen on (sounds) in three phrases of five, seven, and five.

> For example, one of the oldest Japanese haikus:
> *old pond . . .*
> *a frog leaps in*
> *water's sound*

hakuna matata (Swahili) (hah-KOO-nah mah-TAH-tah) (phrase)
There are no worries.

> *Relax. Who cares if that big project is due tomorrow. Sit down. Don't sweat it. HAKUNA MATATA.*

Nota Bene

"Hakuna Matata" was, of course, the title of a hit song from Walt Disney's *The Lion King*. Composed by Alan Menken, with lyrics by Tim Rice, it is the advice Pumbaa and Timon give to the young lion-king-in-exile, Simba. Fortunately at a key turning point in the story, the lioness Nala and the wise old monkey Rafiki come back into the picture to kick some sense into Simba and get him back on the road to recovering his throne.

---

hara kiri (Japanese) (HAH-rah KEE-ree) (noun)
Also known as seppuku, this is a form of ritual suicide. The victim literally disembowels himself with a knife specially reserved for the purpose.

> *Although HARA KIRI was abolished as judicial punishment in 1873, in 1970 several traditionalist Japanese writers committed suicide in this manner.*

hasta la vista (Spanish) (HAHS-tah lah VEES-tah) (phrase)
See you later. It came into widespread use in America following the
1991 film *Terminator 2: Judgment Day*. Who can forget Arnold Schwar-
zenegger's android growling it out, under the tutelage of John Connor?

haute couture (French) (ote koo-TOOR) (noun)
Literally, "high sewing." More generally, the making of high-quality
(and therefore, extremely expensive) clothing to order. This is the
gold standard of fashion and, like most things having to do with
expensive clothing, it's centered in Paris.
>   *Dior and Versace are some examples of the sorts of snooty fashion
>   houses that embody HAUTE COUTURE.*

haute cuisine (French) (ote kwee-ZEEN) (noun)
High-end cooking; food that is prepared using extremely time-
consuming, precise, delicate, and expensive methods—usually for
people who are more interested in how much they spend on a meal
than on what it tastes like.
>   *HAUTE CUISINE is served in the dining room of the hotel where
>   I stayed in New York; that marks me out as someone sophisticated
>   and important.*

hic abundant leones (Latin) (hic ah-BUN-dant lee-OGH-nayz)
(phrase)
Here there abound lions. This phrase was inserted by mapmakers
on those territories that had yet to be explored. It conveyed the idea
of dangers lurking at the edges of the known world. Maps also, on
occasion, warned of cannibals, elephants, and hippos.

hic sunt dracones (Latin) (hic soont drah-KO-nayz) (phrase)
The same as previous, except with dragons. Because *dracones* are
scarier than *leones*.

Hinterland (German) (HIN-ter-lahnd) (noun)
The inland area behind the shoreline of a river or a coastline. More
generally, it refers to a rural area.
>   *When I was little, my family moved from the center of Chicago to
>   the HINTERLAND of Oak Park in the suburbs.*

Hoc signum vincere (Latin) (hok SIG-num WINK-air-ay) (phrase)
Under this sign, conquer. During a period of civil war in the late
Roman Empire, the Emperor Constantine (272–337) faced off
against his opponent, Maxentius, at the Milvian Bridge near Rome.
The night before the battle, a heavenly spirit advised Constantine to
mark his soldiers' shields with a cross, telling him that if he did so,
he would conquer Maxentius. Constantine obeyed the command,
was victorious, and for that reason made Christianity the official
religion of the Roman empire.

hodie mihi, cras tibi (Latin) (HO-dee-ay ME-he kras TI-be)
(phrase)
Literally, "Today to me, tomorrow to you," this phrase refers to the
turn of fortune. This is probably cold comfort to someone who has
just lost a pile of money at the blackjack table in Vegas.
I know I've won every hand for the past two hours, but before you
accuse me of cheating, remember that luck can change. HODIE
MIHI, CRAS TIBI.

hoi polloi (Greek) (HOH-ee pole-OH-ee) (noun)
The many; the majority. Colloquially, the large numbers of lesser-
educated citizens; the Great Unwashed.
I don't feel that my opinions need confirming by the HOI POLLOI;
it's sufficient that I have the support of the educated classes.

hola (Spanish) (HO-lah) (interjection)
Hello! Hi, there!
HOLA, amigo. What's shakin'?

Homines dum docent discunt (Latin) (HAH-min-ayz doom
DOHK-ent DISS-kunt) (phrase)
People learn from teaching. Expresses the pedagogical theory that
the best way to learn something is by teaching it to someone else.
I didn't know how to fly-fish before I was assigned to teach it at
summer camp, but you know what they say: HOMINES DUM
DOCENT DISCUNT.

Homo sum humani a me nihil alienum puto (Latin) (HOH-moh soom hoo-MAN-ee ah may NI-hil AY-lee-num POO-toh) (phrase)
I am a human; thus, nothing human is alien to me. This quotation from the Roman playwright Terence (c. 190–159 B.C.) expresses an idea central to the European Renaissance that any activity of mankind should be a justified subject of study.

H

Honni soit qui mal y pense (French) (O-nee SWA kee mal ee PAHNS) (phrase)
Shame be to him who thinks evil. This French phrase is the motto of the English Order of the Garter. It also appears on the front of British passports.

hora inglesa (Spanish) (HOR-ah in-GLAZ-ah) (noun)
English time. The Spanish phrase implies that punctuality, seen as characteristic of the English, is not very important. The Spanish counterpart is *mañana*, which is literally translated as "tomorrow" but in actuality means "Whenever we get around to it."
He says the windows need to be repaired by the end of today, but he's thinking HORA INGLESA. I think we can do it mañana.

horribile dictu (Latin) (hor-EE-bil-ay DIK-too) (adv.)
Horrible to relate. Prefacing some terrible or distressing statement.
HORRIBILE DICTU, I was laid off from my job today, and, even worse, I found out that my wife is leaving me.

hors de combat (French) (or de kom-BAHT) (adj.)
Literally, "outside the fight." More generally, disabled or unable to continue the battle.
The general's head wound rendered him HORS DE COMBAT at the outset of the fight, which meant he was unable to direct the battle. In his absence, we held the upper hand.

hors d'oeuvre (French) (or DUHVRE) (noun)
Literally, "apart from the main work." A small, bite-sized appetizer served before the commencement of a meal. They are designed to stimulate the appetite and thematically lead into the main course.

houri (Arabic) (HOO-ree) (noun)
Mythical maidens, with modest gazes but of a highly seductive character. Alternately, it is a description of humans who enter paradise after being recreated.

O timeless HOURI, let me enter into the entrancing paradise of your delights!

hubris (Greek) (HYU-briss) (noun)
The quality of overweening pride or overconfidence. The result of this, in Classical Greek literature is invariably **nemesis**, which administers a divine smackdown.

In Sophocles' Antigone, the HUBRIS of Creon, in believing he can substitute his judgment for that of the gods, leads to the death of his son and his prospective daughter-in-law.

"If I speak only one language, I can help my country as only one man. If I can use two languages, I can help as two men. But if I can use all nine languages, then I can work as nine men."

—Village elder, Eritrea

I

ibidem (Latin) (i-BEE-dem) (adv.)
In the same place. Usually abbreviated *ibid*. This refers to a source that was previously cited.

Ich bin ein Berliner (German) (IK bin ayn ber-LIN-er) (phrase)
I am a Berliner. Well, actually, that's what President John F. Kennedy *meant* to say in his 1963 speech, given in West Berlin. One school of thought holds that since *Berliner* means jelly donut, and since the generally accepted way of saying, "I am a citizen of Berlin" is *Ich bin Berliner*, what Kennedy *actually* said was, "I am a donut." Which probably worked just as well as an expression of U.S. foreign policy at the time. To be fair, other interpretations have said that the president's grammar was technically correct.

idée fixe (French) (EE-day FEEKS) (noun)
An obsession or persistent, irrational idea. Such an idea cannot be dislodged by any rational process of argument.
> *As a result of an IDÉE FIXE, some young American women are convinced that they will be able to convince Brad Pitt to break up with Angelina Jolie and move in with them instead. On the other hand, virtually all American men have the same idea about Angelina Jolie.*

idem (Latin) (id-DEM) (adv.)
The same. In citations, refers to a citation that is the same as the one used previously.

id est (Latin) (id EST) (prepositional phrase)
That is. Sometimes abbreviated *i.e.*
> *I am a genius, ID EST, a certified member of Mensa.*

Igitur qui desidera pacem, praeparet bellum (Latin) (IG-i-toor kwi des-EE-dair-ah PAH-kem pre-PI-ret BEL-lum) (phrase)
Therefore, those who desire peace should prepare for war. A comment from Vegetius (c. 383), the author of *Epitoma rei militaris*, a lost treatise on military theory.

ignoratio elenchi (Latin) (ig-nor-AH-tee-oh el-EN-ki) (phrase)
An argument that might be accurate but doesn't address the matter at hand. Much prized by politicians, it is a significant logical fallacy.

To say that because I don't mind higher taxes if they lead to better services means that I must like higher taxes because I'm in a better tax bracket than you is an example of IGNORATIO ELENCHI. You still haven't convinced me.

I

ignotum per ignotius (Latin) (ig-NO-tum pare ig-NO-tee-us) (phrase)
Literally, "the unknown by the more unknown." More generally, it means to give an explanation that is more confusing than the original question.

Your query about the nature of global motion can be answered by a reference to Foucault's Pendulum, with which, of course, everyone is familiar. Or maybe not.

imprimatur (Latin) (im-prim-ah-TOOR) (noun)
An authorization to print something. More colloquially, a stamp of authority.

My pronouncements have the IMPRIMATUR of authority because I'm a recognized expert on, well, everything.

in absentia (Latin) (in ab-SENT-ee-ah) (adv.)
During the absence of. In legal terms, a proceedings in which the accused is not present.

Since the defendant has fled to Canada, this trial will take place IN ABSENTIA, unless his lawyer offers a convincing objection.

in camera (Latin) (in KAH-mare-ah) (adv.)
Secretly. In private. Usually referring to a trial or formal legal hearing that does not admit the public. Although the U.S. Constitution guarantees the right of a public trial, this right is sometimes abridged when matters of national security are invoked. The expression literally means "in the room."

Because the defendants were accused of leaking documents that concerned matters of the highest importance, the entire proceedings were held IN CAMERA.

in extremis (Latin) (in eks-TRAY-mis) (adv.)

Literally, "in extremes"; in the furthest reaches. More generally, in severe conditions up to and including the point of death.

During the snowstorm our body temperatures fell and we had no shelter; we were IN EXTREMIS and therefore, to keep warm, were having sex when the ski patrol found us. That's my story, and I'm sticking to it.

> **Nota Bene**
>
> In 1912, during the race for the South Pole, the English team led by Robert Falcon Scott perished on their return from the pole. Ironically, they had reached their goal some five weeks after their Norwegian rivals, led by Roald Amundsen, had been there. Scott and two others were found months later, frozen in their tent, having died of starvation and exhaustion only eleven miles from a supply depot.

Infinitus est numerus stultorum (Latin) (in-FIN-i-tus est NOO-mare-us stool-TOH-room) (phrase)

The number of stupid people is infinite. From Ecclesiastes 1:15 in the Vulgate. A sentiment with which it's hard to argue, particularly when driving to work in the morning and getting stuck in the right-hand lane behind someone going twenty miles an hour while chattering on a cell phone held in one hand and sipping a latte held in the other, and at the same time presumably steering by pressing his stomach against the wheel.

> **Nota Bene**
>
> The Vulgate translation of the Bible into Latin was made in the late fourth century, mainly by St. Jerome (347–420). It is called the Vulgate from the Latin *vulgare*, meaning "in common usage," since it became the standard and most widely used version of the Bible until the Reformation. Although complete copies of the Vulgate were certainly not rare during the Middle Ages, copies of individual books of the Bible were far more commonplace.

infra dignitatem (Latin) (IN-frah dig-ni-TAH-tem) (adv.)
Beneath one's dignity. Occasionally abbreviated *infra dig.*

> *There's nothing INFRA DIGNITATEM about wearing a costume to a costume party at Halloween, although I agree that going as a sexy French maid vampire in see-through lingerie is probably pushing the limits.*

in loco parentis (Latin) (in LO-ko pahr-EN-tiss) (adv.)
In the place of parents. Referring to someone who serves as a substitute parental figure.

> *Although teachers are often instructed to serve IN LOCO PAREN-TIS, they have little of the authority of parents and are often sued if they attempt to exercise it.*

in medias res (Latin) (in MAY-dee-ahs RAYZ) (adv.)
In the middle of the action. A literary term that refers to opening a scene with the characters in midaction. How they got there is usually explained later via flashbacks.

> *Virgil's* The Aeneid *opens IN MEDIAS RES with the leading characters caught up in a massive storm at sea.*

in memoriam (Latin) (in may-MOH-ree-AHM) (adv.)
In memory of. Often found on grave markers or other symbols of death.

> *IN MEMORIAM Peter Archer, obit. (2012).*

in pace requiescat (Latin) (in PAH-kay RE-kwis-kaht) (adv.)
Rest in peace. A popular sentiment for grave markers.

> *Hic iacet Peter Archer. IN PACE REQUIESCAT.*

in situ (Latin) (in SIT-oo) (adv.)
In place; in its original situation. This concept is particularly important in archaeology and (as anyone who's watched *CSI* is aware) in criminal forensics.

> *Since we suspected foul play once we saw that the skull had been hacked from the body with a machete, we left the skeleton IN SITU.*

inter alia (Latin) (in-tare AHL-ee-ah) (adv.)
Among other things.

I have discovered, INTER ALIA, that you have been using our checking account to pay for liaisons with your old boyfriend.

in toto (Latin) (in TOH-toh) (adv.)
In its entirety.
The hospital bill, IN TOTO, came to $19,574.33. Which seems a bit excessive for having an ingrown toenail removed.

in utero (Latin) (in YOU-tare-oh) (adv.)
Within the uterus. Refers specifically to a baby that is not yet born, although probably still annoying its mother.
When I was IN UTERO, I kicked so much my mother was convinced I was going to be born with a soccer ball.

invicta (Latin) (in-WEEK-tah) (adv.)
Unconquered. The term has been widely used, ranging from the name of a British make of automobile to an early steam locomotive. It's the motto of the county of Kent in England, although you'd think more organizations, possessed of a touching optimism, would make use of it in their mottos.
Until the end of the Vietnam War in 1975, the United States Armed Forces could proudly boast, "INVICTA!" After that, not so much.

in vino veritas (Latin) (in WE-noh WARE-i-tahss) (phrase)
In wine there is truth. Attributed to Pliny the Elder (23–79) as well as to the Greek poet Alcaeus (sixth century B.C.). The idea appears in a number of other languages including Chinese and Hebrew.
When people accuse me of being obnoxious when drunk, I tell them that since IN VINO VERITAS, maybe they just can't handle the truth. Of course, most of the time those people don't invite me to dinner again.

in vitro (Latin) (in WE-troh) (adv.)
Literally, "within a glass." More generally, it refers to experiments that isolate some element of a biological organism to see how it functions. On the other hand, an experiment that is conducted with the organism still *in situ* is referred to as *in vivo*.

ipso facto (Latin) (IP-soh FAK-toh) (phrase)
Literally, "by the fact itself." The more general meaning is something is a direct consequence of something else.

At the party last weekend, I told Mary about the affair her husband was having; but I don't think I'm IPSO FACTO responsible for her subsequently breaking a full bottle of champagne over his head.

I

ius primae noctis (Latin) (YUS PREE-meye NOK-teess) (phrase)
Literally, "the right of first night." This refers to the right, during the Middle Ages, of the Lord of the Manor to take the virginity of a new bride of a peasant living on his land. It's not clear how much this "right" was actually exercised—some historians dismiss it as entirely legendary. In actual fact, the relationship between lord and peasant was a highly complex array of rights and responsibilities on both sides. *Ius primae noctis* is also sometimes referred to as the *droit du seigneur*.

*"Into the face of the young man
who sat on the terrace of the Hotel
Magnifique at Cannes there had
crept a look of furtive shame,
the shifty hangdog look which
announces that an Englishman is
about to talk French."*

—P. G. Wodehouse

J'accuse (French) (ZHAH-kooz) (interjection)
I accuse! This was the title of a famous declaration of the French writer Émile Zola (1840–1902), published on January 13, 1898, declaring his support for Alfred Dreyfus (1859–1935), a French military captain accused of treason. Zola landed in hot water with the government over his declaration and, after being convicted of criminal libel, was forced to flee to England.

Nota Bene
The Dreyfus case, or, as it became known in France, *"l'Affaire,"* was the most notorious judicial proceedings of the nineteenth century. Although Dreyfus was accused of passing military secrets to the German government, it became clear that the French military authorities had accused him out of anti-Semitism and a desire to cover up their own incompetence. Dreyfus was convicted, sent to the penal colony of Devil's Island, granted a new trial, convicted again, and finally, in 1906, exonerated and restored to the military.

Jawohl (German) (yah-VOLE) (interjection)
Yes, sir! I'll get right on that! Normally used when there's an intention to give a military emphasis to something.
JAWOHL, madam! I'll get right on your request for a double latte half caffe with a whisper of cinnamon. Don't let the fact that there are twenty customers in line ahead of you stop you from yelling your order at me.

je ne regrette rien (French) (ZHEH ne re-GRET ree-EHN) (phrase)
I don't regret anything. Most famous as the title of a song recorded by the great French songstress Édith Piaf (1915–1963), dedicated to the French Foreign Legion.

je ne sais pas (French) (ZHEH ne SAY pah) (phrase)
I don't know. The standard answer given by French 101 high school students to any question asked by their teacher. For that matter, the standard answer given by *any* students to *any* question asked by *any* teacher.
You want to know what I'm thinking about? JE NE SAIS PAS. I'm just letting my mind wander.

je ne sais quoi (French) (ZHEH ne say KWAH) (phrase)
Literally, "I don't know what." Colloquially, a kind of inexpressible essence of something, beyond explanation. This is a useful way to convey someone or something's unique character—although not necessarily a good one.

> *I've never tasted anything like this spaghetti sauce before. It has a certain JE NE SAIS QUOI about it. Probably because you added half a bottle of Wild Turkey to it at the last minute.*

J

jeu d'esprit (French) (ZHOO DES-pree) (noun)
A playful spirit. A fun, carefree attitude to life, no matter the stomach-wrenching disasters that may face one.

> *I know your wife has left you and your dog has died, and your company has gone bankrupt and your children have filed a lawsuit against you for spending their inheritance, but I'm sure your JEU D'ESPRIT will carry you through even these difficult times.*

jeunesse dorée (French) (ZHOO-ness dor-AY) (noun)
Wealthy young people who inhabit the upper crust of society. The French equivalent of Paris Hilton, they spend their time hanging out at clubs, summering on the French Riviera, and generally making a significant social nuisance of themselves.

> *The Kardashian family would like to be part of the American JEUNESSE DORÉE, but they don't really have the class to even do that. Which is pretty pathetic, when you think about it.*

jihad (Arabic) (zhee-HAHD) (noun)
One of the most controversial words in the world today, this term refers to the Muslim's religious duty. The literal translation is "struggle," but there is considerable argument, both within and without the Muslim community, over whether this struggle is inherently violent or not. Generally, the term has come to mean a religious war fought by adherents of Islam against nonbelievers.

> *The Taliban and Al Qaeda have conducted a JIHAD against those who disagree with their interpretation of Islam, as well as foreign powers such as the United States.*

> **Nota Bene**
> Part of the confusion over the term *jihad* lies in the fact
> that the Quran seems ambiguous about its meaning. The
> word is not used to refer to fighting in the name of Allah;
> nonetheless, the Prophet Mohammed and his successors
> were clear that Islam must be spread, if necessary through
> war. Though this wasn't very different than the attitude of
> early Christians, who were perfectly comfortable sending
> crusades both against Muslims and to attack and kill her-
> etics within their own ranks.

joie de vivre (French) (ZHWAH de VEEV-reh) (noun)
Literally, "joy in life." A happy attitude toward life; optimism.
   *My friend Melissa is always cheery, even at 6 o'clock in the frickin'
   morning. She's got so much goddamn JOIE DE VIVRE that most
   of her friends want to throttle her.*

"A man who knows two languages is worth two men."

—French proverb

Kaffeeklatsch (German) (KAFF-ay-KLATCH) (noun)
Coffee klatch. Informal discussion or chat. A notable example of German's ability to string a series of words together to produce one monster word.

> *Every morning we gather around the office water cooler to compare notes about how unreasonable the boss was the day before. I just hope he doesn't get word of our little KAFFEEKLATSCH.*

K.

kamikaze (Japanese) (KAH-mi-KAHZ-ee) (noun)
Literally, "divine wind," this was the term for Japanese pilots who crashed their planes into Allied ships in the closing months of World War II. By extension, it has come to mean any suicide attempt in which the suicidal individual attempts to kill not only himself but as many other people as well.

> *Troops in Iraq have been repeatedly subject to KAMIKAZE bombers in the heart of Baghdad.*

karma (Sanskrit) (KAR-mah) (noun)
In Hinduism, this is the notion of an action that causes a series of other actions and reactions, the whole forming a cycle. In general usage, it tends to mean something more akin to the idea that "what goes around, comes around." In other words, you accumulate good karma or bad karma depending on your actions; this karma will eventually result in good or bad things happening to you.

> *I've been opening the door for so many people and helping so many old ladies across the street in the past two weeks that I should have picked up some really good KARMA to balance out that motorcycle I stole.*

Kinder, Kirche, Küche (German) (KIN-der KEERK-e KOOK-e) (phrase) (several alternate versions)
Children, church, kitchen. Although this is now regarded as a reactionary idea, during the period of the rise and triumph of Nazism (1933–1945), it was regarded as the ideal expression of German womanhood. As a phrase, it predated Hitler, but the Nazis believed it perfectly summed up the role of women: to be subordinate to the family, religion, and the state.

kismet (Turkish) (KIZ-met) (noun)
In Persian philosophy, the concept of fate. It has been used as the title of a number of films, as well as a character in the D.C. Comics universe.

KISMET has decreed that we two should meet, have dinner, go back to my house, and make out. Who are we to pit ourselves against fate?

K

kitsch (German) (KITCH) (adj.)
"Art" that is vulgar and tasteless.

Nothing could be more KITSCH than the painting over your bed of Justin Bieber. Unless, of course, it was a picture of Justin Bieber made out of dried pasta. Oh . . . wait . . . sorry. I didn't see what's hanging on the other wall.

klutz (Yiddish) (KLUTZ) (noun)
A clumsy person. The original term in Yiddish meant a lumpy mass, which describes a good many *klutzes* of our acquaintance.

I don't like to do anything involving fine-motor coordination, because I'm such a KLUTZ when it comes to making something by hand. I'm much better at stuff like football.

Kriegspiel (German) (KREEG-shpeel) (noun)
War game. It often refers to a variety of chess invented in 1899 (though it didn't become widely popular). In this variant, the player can see her own pieces but can't see those of her opponent. A referee informs her if a given move is legal or illegal. Not surprisingly, the spread of computers has increased the popularity of this game.

Kulturkampf (German) (KUL-toor-KAHMPF) (noun)
Specifically, this term, translated as "culture struggle," refers to the anti-Catholic campaign waged by Prussian politician Otto von Bismarck (1815–1898) against the Catholic Church. More generally, it refers to any cultural conflict that has strong political overtones.

Since the 1980s, the Republican Party in the United States has waged a KULTURKAMPF over such issues as gay marriage and school textbooks. At least on the issue of gay marriage, it appears to be losing.

Nota Bene

The issue of cultural struggle was closely linked to politics in Germany. Adolf Hitler was a violent opponent of what he regarded as "degenerate tendencies" in modern art. After his rise to power, in 1937 the Nazi government organized a display of such art to show the German people what they were fighting against. Unfortunately for the Nazis, the exhibit, which included paintings by such modern masters as Marc Chagall, Pablo Picasso, Vincent van Gogh, and Max Beckmann, drew unprecedented numbers of viewers, and the Nazis hastily closed the exhibit.

*"To use two languages familiarly
and without contaminating one by
the other, is very difficult; and to use
more than two is hardly to be hoped.
The prizes which some have received
for their multiplicity of languages
may be sufficient to excite industry,
but can hardly generate confidence."*

—Samuel Johnson

L

Labor omnia vincit (Latin) (LAH-bor OHM-nee-ah WIN-kit) (phrase)

Hard work conquers all. From the *Georgics* by Virgil (70 B.C–19 B.C.), this expresses a typically Roman attitude; not that all Romans followed it in practice. In practice, what the motto really meant was, "Hard work by slaves and the Plebians conquers all so that we, the Senators and the upper class, can lie around on our couches drinking wine and eating grapes and occasionally overthrowing the emperor."

laissez faire (French) (LEH-say FARE) (adj.)

Literally, "leave it be." Generally applied as an economic term, specifying a philosophy according to which the economy should be free from government control or interference, allowing market forces to work out all problems. This school of thought is most associated with Adam Smith (1723–1790) and his book *The Wealth of Nations* (1776). However, Smith did not use the phrase, and it's doubtful that a close reading of his works would support the idea that he was a laissez-faire economist—at lease in the sense that the term is used today.

> *It seems to me that if the government would practice LAISSEZ FAIRE, the economy would work just fine. And if I become fabulously rich as a result, well, that's obviously the way things were meant to be.*

lapsus linguae (Latin) (LAP-soos LING-why) (noun)

A slip of the tongue.

> *I meant to say, "Let's table the resolution," but in a LAPSUS LINGUAE I accidentally said, "Let's table the revolution."*

Nota Bene

Sigmund Freud (1856–1939) presented the idea in his 1901 book *The Psychopathology of Everyday Life* that many slips of the tongue are, in fact, a key to understanding the unconscious mind of the speaker. Today, the term "Freudian slip" (which Freud never used) is applied to pretty much any slip of the tongue.

Lebensraum (German) (LAY-benz-rowm) (noun)
Living space. In the 1930s, Adolf Hitler (1889–1945) came to power in Germany by appealing to the nationalist instincts of the German people. Above all, he argued, the Germans needed *Lebensraum*, room to expand to the east into what Hitler argued were traditionally German lands such as Poland and Czechoslovakia.

Lederhosen (German) (LAY-der-HOZ-en) (noun)
Leather shorts, either knee-length or shorter, usually supported by two shoulder straps. They originated in the Alpine regions of Germany in Bavaria. Although still worn in those areas, their popularity has declined in the rest of Germany.
> *Even though we're going to a beer festival, I don't think it was necessary for you to wear LEDERHOSEN and a Tyrolean hat with a feather in it.*

Leitmotif (German) (LAYT-moh-TEEF) (noun)
Leading motif. Originally a musical term, though it is sometimes also applied to literature. It refers to a recurring theme that is associated with a person, place, or idea.
> *In Prokofiev's* Peter and the Wolf, *the LEITMOTIF of Peter is signaled by the orchestra's string section.*

lèse-majesté (French) (LEHZ MAH-zhess-tay) (noun)
An offense against the reigning monarch or ruler of a state. More generally, an offense committed against some significant power, either in a state or an organization.
> *For you to slap the CEO on the back and call him by his first name was an impermissible act of LÈSE-MAJESTÉ. Please clear out your desk and exit the building.*

lex talionis (Latin) (LEX tal-ee-OH-neess) (noun)
Literally, "law of the talon." More colloquially, the principle of "an eye for an eye"—he who injures a person shall receive the same injury. This concept of law dates back to the reign of the Babylonian monarch Hammurabi (d. 1750 B.C.), whose laws were engraved on a series of *stelae*. To a great extent, it has disappeared from Western jurisprudence.

You took my cocktail, so, in accordance with LEX TALONIS, I'm going to take yours. And I'll take your date along with it.

Liebchen (German) (LEEB-chen) (noun)
Sweetheart; dear. A term of affection, usually applied by a grownup to a child.
Come here, LIEBCHEN, and give your grandmother a nice hug and kiss.

lingua franca (Latin) (LING-wah FRANK-ah) (noun)
A language that makes it possible for people who don't share the same linguistic background to communicate with one another.
Today, especially in business, English is the LINGUA FRANCA of the Western world.

Nota Bene
There have been many attempts to create a universal language, but among the most ambitious was Esperanto. This constructed language was created by L. L. Zamenhof in 1887 in an attempt to transcend national borders and political disputes. Two world wars, one cold war, two atomic bombs, and many many regional conflicts later, it's safe to say that Zamenhof was hopelessly optimistic in his plans for Esperanto. Nevertheless, it is estimated that today up to 2 million people are fluent in this language.

loco citato (Latin) (LOH-ko kee-TAH-toh) (adv.)
Literally, "in the place cited." In bibliographic citation, this refers to the previous place in the footnotes or endnotes in which a particular word was referred to.

locum tenens (Latin) (LOH-kum TEN-enz) (noun)
Placeholder. Someone who temporarily does a job in place of someone else. The term is particularly applied to the medical and teaching professions.
Because Dr. Appleforth is, unfortunately, appearing before the medical board on charges of malpractice due to constant drunkenness, I

am his LOCUM TENENS. And I hope you'll feel more comfortable with me taking out your spleen than you would have with him.

louche (French) (LOOSH) (adj.)
Of questionable taste. In bad taste.

I think that for you to wear a Party Naked and Drink tee shirt to a meeting of Alcoholics Anonymous is LOUCHE—to put it mildly.

"You live a new life for every new language you speak."

—Czech proverb

M

magister dixit (Latin) (mah-GIS-tare DEEKS-it) (phrase)
The teacher has said it. Although the teacher originally referred to by this medieval saying was Aristotle, it can be applied to anyone considered an irreproachable authority.

> *Stephen Hawking argues for the existence of black holes at the center of every galaxy, and since MAGISTER DIXIT, I'm inclined to go along with this argument.*

magna cum laude (Latin) (MAG-nah koom LAW-day) (adv.)
With great praise. A qualification of an academic degree. One can achieve a degree by itself; with praise (see **cum laude**); with great praise; or with highest praise (see **summa cum laude**).

> *My daughter has just graduated from Wellesley College MAGNA CUM LAUDE with a degree in medieval philosophy. I wonder how long it'll be before she's back living at home.*

magnum opus (Latin) (MAG-noom OH-pus) (noun)
Literally, "great work." The most important or significant production of one's career. Although it usually refers to a written work, it isn't necessarily restricted to that.

> *I consider Samuel Johnson's* A Dictionary of the English Language *to be his MAGNUM OPUS, one for which he's still justly celebrated.*

mala fides (Latin) (MAH-lah FEED-days) (adv.)
In bad faith. See **bona fides**.

> *Throughout this entire affair, I consider that you have been acting in MALA FIDES, and therefore I'm breaking off our partnership and going to the police with my concerns about your business practices. And you can just put down that crowbar, because you don't scare me at all.*

mal de mer (French) (MAHL de MARE) (noun)
Seasickness. Feeling as if you're going to lose your lunch over the side of the boat sounds much more impressive if you can say it in French.

> *Even though the weather was calm and we were steering a clear course for the island, half the passengers were below decks suffering from MAL DE MER.*

mañana (Spanish) (mahn-YAH-nah) (noun/adv.)
Literally, "tomorrow." However, the more general meaning of this phrase is, "Whenever I get around to doing it, which could be tomorrow but equally could be next week, next month, next year, or never."

There's no need to worry about that hole in the roof. It's probably not hurting anything. I'll fix it MAÑANA.

mano a mano (Spanish) (MAH-no ah MAH-no) (adv.)
Literally, "hand to hand." More generally, man to man. One on one. There's a degree of machismo implied in this concept, that two big, sweaty, and possibly somewhat stupid men will stand face to face and slug out some dispute.

My beer is better than your beer, and I'll go MANO A MANO with you to prove it.

ma non troppo (Italian) (MAH non TROH-poh) (adj.)
Not too much. Not excessive.

This passage is marked Allegro MA NON TROPPO, so don't play it overly fast.

manqué (French) (man-KAY) (noun)
Literally, "to miss." In general, someone or something who hasn't lived up to expectations.

Although my friend graduated summa cum laude from Harvard and was a member of the best law firm in the country, he's a bit of a legal MANQUÉ; he spends all of his time now soliciting hit-and-run insurance cases.

mantra (Sanskrit) (MAHN-trah) (noun)
In Hinduism, a word or group of words that is chanted in an effort to create a spiritual transformation. In English usage, it means an overriding theme or idea that's expressed over and over again, usually until everyone within earshot is sick and tired of it.

The MANTRA of the Obama presidential administration has been Hope and Change.

mare nostrum (Latin) (MAH-ray NOS-trum) (phrase)
Literally, "our sea." The way Romans (and other southern Europeans) referred to the Mediterranean Sea. Sometimes used to indicate something that's considered a possession held in common by a number of people.

M

> *Although we tend to view our town fire department as MARE NOSTRUM, in fact it's actually a private company, so we don't have any real control over what it does.*

matériel (French) (mah-TARE-ee-ell) (noun)
Literally, "equipment" or "hardware." More commonly, it refers to military supplies.

> *We'll be able to hold this position against the enemy, provided that we have an adequate supply of men and MATÉRIEL.*

maven (Yiddish) (MAY-ven) (noun)
Someone whose expertise in a particular area is widely trusted. A teacher.

> *I can say, with all modesty, that I am a bit of a MAVEN in a number of areas, including philosophy, the arts, literature, mathematics, and string saving. But enough about me.*

mazel tov (Yiddish) (MAH-zell toff) (interjection)
Good luck; congratulations.

> *I hear your son just graduated from dental school. MAZEL TOV!*

mea culpa (Latin) (MAY-ah KUL-pah) (interjection)
I am to blame. It's my fault.

> *Since I was responsible for the accounting error that inadvertently caused the bank to pay $1.8 million into my personal bank account, I suppose some sort of MEA CULPA is in order. Not that I'm admitting any legal accountability, mind you.*

Media vita in morte sumus (Latin) (MAY-dee-ah WE-tah in MOR-tay SOO-moos) (phrase)
In the midst of life, we are in death. A popular motto on gravestones, it probably originated in early medieval France. It also pops up, appropriately enough, in Bram Stoker's 1897 novel *Dracula*.

Meistersinger (German) (MEYE-stir-zing-er) (noun)
Literally, "master singer." In Germany in the late Middle Ages, singers and poets were members of urban associations called guilds. A member of one of these guilds was referred to as a Meistersinger. In 1868, Richard Wagner (1813–1883) composed *Die Meistersinger von Nürnberg*, considered to be among his most important works.

M

> **Nota Bene**
>
> Wagner was a notorious anti-Semite, something that no doubt contributed to the attraction Hitler felt for his works. The unfortunate result (as well as the fact that several of Wagner's descendants were publicly associated with the Nazis) has been to link Wagner and Nazism in the public mind. In 1995, Wagner's opera *The Flying Dutchman* was broadcast in Israel, marking the first time the composer's music was publicly heard in the Jewish state.

mélange (French) (may-LAHNZH) (noun)
Random mixture of things.
> *The interior of your house is a sort of MÉLANGE of furniture styles, ranging from Victorian to the steel-and-chrome constructs of the 1970s.*

memento mori (Latin) (me-MEN-toh MOR-ee) (phrase)
Literally, "Remember your mortality." In art, this refers to a genre of art, popular in the Middle Ages, the purpose of which was to emphasize human mortality and the vanity of human aspirations.
> *Walking through a cemetery, for me, serves as a MEMENTO MORI.*

ménage à trois (French) (may-NAZH ah TWAH) (noun)
A sexual encounter involving three people at the same time. Every man's ideal Christmas present but one that is, alas, rarely found under the tree.
> *I was involved in a MÉNAGE À TROIS several years ago, but it got complicated when one of the women's Hell's Angels boyfriend showed up unexpectedly.*

Mens sana in corpore sano (Latin) (mens SAH-na in kor-POR-ay SAN-oh) (phrase)
A sound mind in a healthy body. The sort of thing personal trainers are apt to say to their clients in the midst of a particularly rough session at the gym.

meshugga (Yiddish) (meh-SHUG-gah) (adj.)
Crazy; insane.
> *That girl, she's a little MESHUGGA where men are concerned. She needs to settle down and meet a nice boy. Maybe my brother's nephew would do.*

mi casa es su casa (Spanish) (ME KAH-sa ess SOO KAH-sah) (phrase)
Literally, "My house is your house." Generally, you're welcome in my home; treat it as if it were your own.
> *I want you to feel completely at home here. MI CASA ES SU CASA. Just take off your shoes before you come in. And wash your hands before touching anything. And don't use any of the towels; you might get marks on them.*

mirabile visu (Latin) (mir-AH-bee-lay WE-zoo) (adv.)
Wonderful to see.
> *You know our 300-pound neighbor? Yesterday when I was out jogging, MIRABILE VISU I saw him as well. Of course, he was wearing lime green spandex, so now I'll have to claw my face off.*

moi non plus (French) (MWAH non ploo) (phrase)
Me neither. It was part of the title of a well-known French pop song, "Je t'aime . . . moi non plus," sung as a duet by Serge Gainsbourg and sex bomb Brigitte Bardot in 1967. For its time, it was considered scandalous and was banned in the U.K., with the not-unexpected result that every British teenager knew the words by heart.

mise en place (French) (MEEZ ohn plass) (noun)
An assembly of all the various prepared bits and pieces of a recipe. The cook places them within easy reach so they can be added to the cooking process as needed.

*I'm making chicken crepes this evening, so your job is to prepare a
MISE EN PLACE for me and then get out of my way. Then eat the
food and tell me how wonderful it is.*

mise en scène (French) (MEEZ ohn seen) (phrase)
Literally, "placing on stage." This has become a technical term, especially
in film, for the visual elements of the movie that are used to tell the story.
> *In the classic movie* Battleship Potemkin, *director Sergei Eisenstein
> used montages and fast cutaways as his MISE EN SCÈNE.*

modus operandi (Latin) (MOH-dus op-er-AN-dee) (noun)
Method of operation. Characteristic mode of proceeding with
something.
> *Richard Nixon's MODUS OPERANDI in almost any situation
> was to first lie, then cover up the lie, and then to cover up the cover-up.*

modus vivendi (Latin) (MOH-dus we-WEN-dee) (noun)
Method of living; lifestyle.
> *I've found that the MODUS VIVENDI that works best for me is
> overindulgence in eating, drinking, and sexual activity. So I'm just
> going with the flow.*

montage (French) (mon-TAZH) (noun)
A collection of images, placed together. In film, these images are shown
quickly, one after the other. Musical elements and special effects may also
contribute to the sense of energy and change that such filming brings.
> *Modern filmmakers often use a technique of MONTAGE to suggest
> the passage of time.*

Nota Bene
In 1982, in the film *Koyaanisqatsi: Life Out of Balance*,
director Godfrey Reggio made a comment on the frentic
and dysfunctional character of modern urban existence.
Using combinations of montage, time-lapse photography,
and dramatic slow motion, he depicted life in urban centers
as out of touch with the natural rhythms that humans have
followed for centuries. The title of the film is from a word
in the Hopi language meaning "unbalanced life."

M

Morituri te salutant (Latin) (mor-i-TOO-ree tay sal-oo-TANT) (phrase) (several versions)
Those who are about to die salute you. According to the Roman historian Suetonius (c. 69–c. 130) it was with this phrase that Roman gladiators greeted the emperor as they entered the arena. There are variations to the phrase in other accounts, and although it may have been used once or twice, it's by no means clear that it was a standard greeting.

mortuum flagellas (Latin) (mor-TOO-oom flah-GEL-lass) (phrase)
You're beating the dead. Equivalent to the more colloquial "beating a dead horse."
I don't see why you keep harping on the fact that I slept with your best friend right after the wedding. It seems a case of MORTUUM FLAGELLAS to me.

mos maiorum (Latin) (mos my-OH-rum) (phrase)
The customs of our ancestors. Generally, since the Romans revered age and equated it with wisdom, this term was intended to show that something had the force of ancient custom behind it and should not be disturbed.
The prohibition against selling alcohol on Sunday morning has the power of MOS MAIORUM, and I see no reason to disturb it by new legislation.

mot juste (French) (moh zhust) (noun)
The right, or proper, word. For the French, who obsess over matters of language to a considerably greater degree than other nations, finding the right word for every occasion is of the utmost importance. And, if they can't find the right one, they make one up—as long as it doesn't bear any resemblance to an American expression.
In my writing, I always strive to find the MOT JUSTE to refine my communications with the masses.

mutatis mutandis (Latin) (moo-TAH-tees moo-TAHN-dees) (phrase)

The necessary changes having been made.

I'd like you to re-examine these figures, MUTATIS MUTANDIS, and see whether they bear out my contention that there is scientific proof that pheromone production increases exponentially for each shot of tequila after the first three.

"One who speaks only one language is one person, but one who speaks two languages is two people."

—Turkish proverb

Natura non facit saltus (Latin) (nah-TOO-rah non FAH-kit SAHL-tus) (phrase)
Nature does not make leaps. This principle was upheld by scientists from the time of Aristotle, expressing the idea that many changes occur gradually. Although it was also a principle of the theory of evolution posed by Charles Darwin (1809–1882), it has been challenged in recent years by such evolutionary biologists as Stephen Jay Gould (1941–2002) in his theory of punctuated equilibrium.

née (French) (nay) (adv.)
Born. Referring, usually, to a woman's maiden name.
> *The wife of John F. Kennedy was Jacqueline Kennedy NÉE Jacqueline Bouvier.*

nemesis (Greek) (NEH-mis-sis) (noun)
A negative fate, the outcome of overweening pride (see **hubris**). Anyone, the ancient Greeks believed, who tried to rise above what the gods had decreed for them would be brought down by the gods. This was a governing principle of Greek drama, exemplified by such plays as *Antigone* and *Oedipus the King* by Sophocles (c. 497 B.C.–406 B.C.). Nemesis is the agent of such divine retribution.
> *Because you boasted of your vast sexual prowess, it's only right that your NEMESIS should take the form of an STD.*

Nemo igitur vir magnus sine aliquo adflatu divino umquam fuit (Latin) (NAY-mo ig-i-TOOR weer MAG-nus sin-AY AH-lee-kwo ad-FLAT-oo di-WE-no OOM-kwahm FOO-it) (phrase)
There was never a great man, save through divine inspiration. A quotation from Marcus Tullius Cicero (106 B.C.–43 B.C.), from his book *De Natura Deorum* (*On the Nature of the Gods*).

Nota Bene
A master of Latin prose, Cicero was also a self-regarding, persnickety, argumentative member of the Roman upper classes. He was a member of the Senate and sharply opposed the rise of Julius Caesar (100 B.C.–44 B.C.). Following the reaction after Caesar's murder and the triumph of Marc Anthony (83 B.C.–30 B.C.), Cicero was murdered by Anthony's supporters.

Nemo me impune laecesit (Latin) (NAY-moh MAY im-POON lie-KES-it) (phrase)
No one touches me with impunity. This is the motto of several Scottish regiments of the British Army, confirming that no one in their right mind should make fun of a Scot wearing a kilt.

N

ne plus ultra (Latin) (neh ploos UL-trah) (phrase)
Nothing further than; nothing beyond. The Romans used this phrase to refer to the perceived geographical limitations of their world. Beyond the Mediterranean and into the Atlantic Ocean, for example, their knowledge did not extend.
> *Your knowledge of geography is the NE PLUS ULTRA. Regarding pretty much everything else, you don't know what you're talking about.*

n'est-ce pas (French) (ness PAH) (phrase)
Isn't that the case? A French question that expects the answer to be affirmative.
> *Going out with me is probably the most delightful experience you've had in many months, N'EST-CE PAS?*

nicht wahr (German) (nikt vahr) (phrase)
Isn't that the case? Again, this expects an affirmative reply.
> *All citizens should obey the traffic laws, even if you're stopped at a red light at midnight and there's no one else around, NICHT WAHR?*

Nihil boni sine labore (Latin) (NEE-hil BOH-nee SI-neh lah-BOR-ay) (phrase)
Nothing worthwhile is achieved without work. The motto of several schools, although you'd think it's a sentiment that would be more widespread than it is. God knows, it's the kind of thing parents are always saying to their children, usually without any effect whatever.

nil admirari (Latin) (nil ad-mir-RAH-ree) (phrase)
Nothing astonishes me. Nothing bothers me. The phrase has been variously attributed to Cicero (106 B.C.–43 B.C.) and to Horace (65

B.C.–8 B.C.). It expresses a widely admired Roman virtue: To let nothing disturb one's fortitude.

> *Despite the collapse of my banking empire, NIL ADMIRARI. I face the future with an equitable spirit—including my court date next week.*

nil desperandum (Latin) (nil des-per-AND-doom) (interjection)
Don't despair.

> *It's true that our customers hate our products, our accountant was just convicted of embezzlement, and our warehouse just burned to the ground. But NIL DESPERANDUM! I'm sure something will turn up.*

noblesse oblige (French) (NO-bless oh-BLEEZH) (adv.)
Literally, "Nobility obliges." More generally, the idea that privilege includes responsibilities, although this concept has not, perhaps, been much in evidence in recent years.

> *Because of my vast wealth, I like to spend every Christmas day in a soup kitchen, dispensing warm meals to those less fortunate. NOBLESSE OBLIGE, you know.*

Noli me tangere (Latin) (NOH-lee may TAHN-geh-reh) (phrase)
Touch me not. According to the Gospel of John, this is what Jesus said to Mary Magdalene when she recognized him after his resurrection. The moment has been the subject of numerous works of art, and it's suggested that a more accurate translation of the biblical Greek might be, "Stop clinging to me."

nolle prosequi (Latin) (NO-lay pro-SEK-we) (interjection)
Literally, "Don't follow." More generally, in a criminal case it means "Don't prosecute." In general conversation, it means, as P. G. Wodehouse (1881–1975) once said, "Nuts to you."

> *When John and Janet asked me to help them move to a new house, I thought about the last time I agreed to help them move, and the fact that they hadn't packed anything by the day of the move. With that in mind, I extended a firm NOLLE PROSEQUI.*

nolo contendere (Latin) (NO-loh kon-TEN-der-ay) (phrase)
I don't want to contend; I don't want to contest. This is a form of legal pleading, referred to as a plea of no contest. It means the

defendant accepts the sentence of the court without actually pleading guilty or not guilty.

> **Nota Bene**
>
> The concept of *nolo contendere* became widely known in
> the United States—more widely, at any rate, than it had
> previously been—in 1973 when Vice President Spiro
> Agnew (1918–1996) pleaded no contest in a bribery trial.
> The plea was accepted by the court with the condition that
> he resign as vice president. He was replaced by Gerald Ford
> (1913–2006), who became president when Richard Nixon
> (1913–1994) resigned the presidency in August 1974.

nom de guerre (French) (nahm de GAIR) (noun)
Literally, "war name." Generally a name that is assumed in times
of stress or conflict. Traditionally, such names were adopted by
soldiers in the French army in the seventeenth and eighteenth
centuries, often based on the soldier's place of origin.

> *In the twentieth century, the Russian revolutionary Vladimir
> Ilyich Ulyanov adopted the NOMME DE GUERRE "Lenin."*

nom de plume (French) (nahm de PLOOM) (noun)
Pen name. The name under which authors sometimes choose to write.

> *The English mathematician Charles Dodgson wrote under
> the NOM DE PLUME Lewis Carroll, producing the masterpieces*
> Alice in Wonderland *and* Alice Through the Looking-Glass.

> **Nota Bene**
>
> There have been many famous noms de plume throughout
> history. For example, the Englishman Eric Blair (1903–
> 1950) is much better known as George Orwell. Mary Anne
> Evans (1819–1880) wrote her masterpieces under the
> name George Eliot, and the French writer François-Marie
> Arouet (1694–1778) has come down to us under his *nom de
> plume* of Voltaire. In fact, aspiring young writers might well
> be advised that the first thing they should do when launch-
> ing their careers is cast about for a suitable pseudonym.

non compos mentis (Latin) (non KOM-pos MEN-tees) (phrase)
Not of sound mind; crazy; wacko; the choo-choo train having chugged right off the tracks.

> *I'd pay more attention to Benedict's business advice, but from what I can tell from his behavior lately, he's NON COMPOS MENTIS. At any rate, I don't think it's normal for a man to wear Speedos and a tee shirt to the office.*

non scholae, sed vitae discimus (Latin) (non SKOHL-eye sed WE-tie DIS-ki-mus) (phrase)
We do not learn for school but for life. A phrase that generally means one should study for real life and not just to pass tests. More or less the opposite philosophy of the No Child Left Behind Act.

non sequitur (Latin) (non SEK-wit-oor) (noun)
Literally, "that which does not follow." Something that has no obvious connection to what was said or written previously.

> *When I told you I was getting married, your response of, "We had spaghetti at our house three times last week," confused me, since it was a NON SEQUITUR.*

Nosce te ipsum (Latin) (NOS-keh tay IP-sum) (phrase)
Know yourself. Used by Thomas Hobbes (1558–1679) in his book *Leviathan*; its pedigree stretches back to ancient Greece. The American poet and essayist Ralph Waldo Emerson (1803–1882) made it the title of a poem, in which he suggested that to know oneself was to know God.

nota bene (Latin) (NO-tah BEN-ay) (interjection)
Note well. Pay attention.

> *I'm going to give you a piece of very good advice. NOTA BENE: When someone asks you to give an opinion on a book they've written, run. Run far.*

nouveaux riche (French) (NOO-voh REESH) (noun)
Newly wealthy. The term carries a strong implication that newly earned money is less classy than old money and that the Nouveaux riche as a social class are vulgar and tasteless.

We don't believe in inviting the NOUVEAUX RICHE to our Christmas parties; they'd probably come wearing fake fur or some other tacky thing. If you haven't inherited your fortune, you're not welcome in our home.

nouvelle cuisine (French) (NOO-vell kwe-ZINE) (noun)
Literally, "new dining." A culinary movement that arose in the 1970s, first among French chefs such as Michel Guérard (1933–). The principles of the movement were that food should be simple, cooked less to preserve the natural flavors, and that there should be a strong "artistic" element in the presentation.

In practice, this led to chefs putting a prawn and six peas on a plate with two paintbrush strokes of white sauce and a sprig of parsley, then charging $36 for it. Fortunately, most chefs came back from the Dark Side, and *nouvelle cuisine* is largely only a horrid memory.

novus ordo seclorum (Latin) (NO-vus OR-doh sek-LOH-room) (phrase)
New order of the ages. This phrase appears on the dollar bill beneath a pyramid topped with an all-seeing eye—a fact that has stimulated all sorts of conspiracy theories about the Freemasons, the Illuminati, the New World Order, and the Trilateral Commission. For a novel based on these theories, see Dan Brown's *The Lost Symbol*. For a *good* novel based on these theories, see Umberto Eco's *Foucault's Pendulum*.

nudnik (Yiddish) (NUD-nik) (noun)
A stupid, boring oaf.
I can't believe your mother seated me next to Cousin Mordecai. He's such a NUDNIK; I was asleep at the table halfway through dinner.

nunc dimittis (Latin) (nunk DIM-i-tis) (phrase)
Now let him depart. The phrase, which appears in Luke 2:29, is the title of a Christian hymn.

Nunc scio quid sit amor (Latin) (nunk SKEE-oh kwid sit AH-mor) (phrase)

Now I know what love means. A line from the *Eclogues* by Virgil (70 B.C.–19 B.C.). The line can be romantic or ironic, depending on your need. On the chance that the person you're talking to doesn't know Latin, it's as well to have a translation handy.

"Knowledge of languages is the doorway to wisdom."

—Roger Bacon

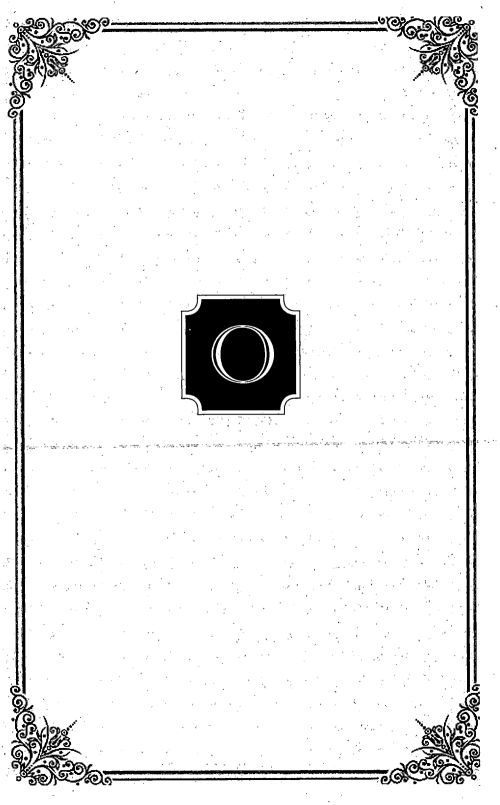

obiter dictum (Latin) (OH-bit-tur DIK-toom) (adv.)
Said in passing.

> *My good friend is entirely mistaken in his argument, OBITER DICTUM one that I have heard many times before from others more educated than he, that the property lines of our town intersect with those of our neighbors.*

objet d'art (French) (ahb-ZHAY dart) (noun)
A work of art. Usually not a painting or sculpture but something that has other uses but can be considered a work of art.

> *The museum has recently acquired a fine collection of silver urns, cups, spoons, and other OBJETS D'ART that are now on display in the main gallery.*

objet trouvé (French) (ahb-ZHAY troo-VAY) (noun)
Something that has been found. In this context, it refers to a type of art made from non-art-related objects. For example, a sculpture made of popsicle sticks might reasonably claim to be an objet trouvé.

> **Nota Bene**
> One of the leaders of the "Found Art" movement was Marcel Duchamp (1887–1968), one of the originators of Dadaism. This school of art attempted to parody existing styles and to push art out of its standard boundaries. Duchamp, for instance, shocked the art world in 1917 when he exhibited a urinal, titling it "Fountain."

Oktoberfest (German) (ahk-TOH-ber-fest) (noun)
A festival in Bavaria, Germany, characterized by large amounts of drinking. Since this is Germany we're talking about, we perhaps should say larger amounts of drinking. Traditionally it runs from late September through the first part of October. It has spread to many other parts of the world, and in the United States many craft brewers bring out Oktoberfest beers in celebration.

Omnia mutantur, nihil interit (Latin) (OHM-nee-ah moo-TAHN-toor NI-hil IN-tare-it) (phrase)

Everything changes but nothing is completely lost. A comment, appropriately enough from the *Metamorphoses* of Ovid (43 B.C.– A.D. 17).

Nota Bene
The Romans may have tried to project an image of puritan dedication to emperor and state, but they liked a dirty story as well as anybody. Ovid got in a good deal of trouble with the first Roman emperor, Augustus (63 B.C.–A.D. 14) and was banished in A.D. 8, almost certainly because some of his poems were deemed "immoral." The not-surprising result was that Romans—and legions of schoolboys up through the nineteenth century—read Ovid's poetry eagerly, searching for salacious meanings.

omnia praesumuntur legitime facta donec probentur in contrarium (Latin) (AHM-nee-ah pry-zu-MUNT-oor lay-GIT-i-may FAK-tah DON-ek pro-BEN-toor in kon-TRA-ree-um) (phrase)
A legal term, meaning all things are legitimately done until proven otherwise. In other words, if something is not explicitly forbidden by law, it can be presumed to be legal.

omnium gatherum (Latin) (AHM-nee-um GA-ther-um) (noun)
A miscellaneous collection; a hodge-podge.
My study is an OMNIUM GATHERUM of detritus, accumulated from the different stages of my intellectual development.

opus citatum (Latin) (OH-pus ki-TAH-tum) (phrase)
Literally, "The work having been cited." Usually abbreviated *op. cit.* in footnotes and bibliography, it refers the reader to the previous citation of the work in a different place in the book or article.

O tempora, o mores (Latin) (oh TEM-por-ah oh MOR-ayz) (phrase)
Our dreadful times! Our horrible customs! This gloomy sentiment is from a speech by Cicero (106 B.C.–43 B.C.) denouncing his rival Catiline (108 B.C.–62 B.C.). Catiline was, in Cicero's view, attempting to overthrow the Roman Republic, and Cicero's speech, in consequence, dealt with the decline of Roman virtue from the Good Old

Days to his time. The expression can be employed by anyone wishing to suggest that things used to be much better than they are now.

oy gevalt (Yiddish) (OY gh-VAHLT) (interjection)
Literally, "Oh, pain!" This expression is meant to suggest negative surprise or dismay.

You mean we're going to Uncle Seymour's for Chanukah this year? OY GEVALT! He drives me crazy!

oy vey (Yiddish) (OY VAY) (interjection)
Another Yiddish comment that means pretty much the same as **oy gevalt** and can be used interchangeably. The Jewish people have had a lot to be dismayed and exasperated about in their history, so it's understandable that Yiddish is full of expressions like this.

What do you mean, you didn't make the maror for the Seder? OY VEY! How could you forget something like that?

"A different language is a different vision of life."

—Federico Fellini

panem et circenses (Latin) (pan-em et keer-KEN-seez) (phrase)
Literally, "bread and circuses." Generally, any large spectacle staged by the state in order to distract the masses of people from more important issues. The phrase was first used by the Roman writer Juvenal (first century A.D.).

Because the senator knew his marital problems would create an electoral problem for him, he tried to woo people away from the camp of his opponent with PANEM ET CIRCENSES such as a giant barbeque.

Nota Bene
The word "circus" in the context of Roman society does not mean something involving elephants and trapeze artists and so on. Rather, it refers to the circular or oval arenas in which races were staged. Thus "circus" is from the same root as our word "circular." This can be seen in modern London, where traffic roundabouts are called circuses (e.g., Piccadilly Circus).

papier-mâché (French) (PAP-ee-ay MA-shay) (noun)
A sculpted form made by covering a wire frame with strips of paper soaked in a paste solution. The structure, when dry, can be painted or additionally carved. The process dates back at least to ancient Egypt.

We made masks for the ball out of PAPIER-MÂCHÉ and painted them in garish colors, as well as decorating them with feathers.

par avion (French) (par ah-vee-OHN) (adv.)
By air. A stamp placed on the outside of airmail envelopes to ensure proper sorting. This, of course, was back when there *was* such a thing as air mail instead of the ubiquitous e-mail.

par excellence (French) (pahr eks-sell-AHNS) (adv.)
To perfection. Literally, "by excellence." This can be applied to a person, place, or thing that embodies the spirit of something.

Paris Hilton is the empty-headed socialite PAR EXCELLENCE. In fact, that's really the only thing she's excellent at.

pari passu (Latin) (PAH-ree PAS-soo) (adv.)
On equal footing. Sometimes, it is used in investing circles to refer to two or more assets that are considered equally.

> *Although George and I trained in two different events for this meet, we are PARI PASSU in the eyes of the spectators. That said, I plan to win my event; I'm not so sure about him.*

P

passe-partout (French) (PAHS-par-too) (noun)
A pass key. Something that provides universal entry or passage.

> *Although I've forgotten my room key, the concierge has been good enough to supply a PASSE-PARTOUT to enable us to gain entrance.*

Nota Bene
The novel *Around the World in Eighty Days* by Jules Verne (1828–1905) includes a French character named Passepartout, the assistant to the intrepid English hero, Phileas Fogg. While Fogg marches unmoved through perils that include an angry Hindu mob, political brawlers in San Francisco, and a band of rampaging Indians in the American west, it is Passepartout who usually fixes problems and in the end enables Mr. Fogg to successfully complete his quest.

passim (Latin) (PAS-sim) (adv.)
Here, there, and everything. In citations, this means that a particular term is found throughout the cited text.

pastiche (French) (pahs-TEESH) (noun)
A hodge-podge. A collection of things, randomly assembled. It can also refer to an imitation of something, usually not intended to be taken seriously.

> *There are dozens, if not hundreds, of PASTICHES of the Sherlock Holmes stories, but none comes close to the genius of the original tales by Sir Arthur Conan Doyle.*

pater familias (Latin) (PAH-tare fah-MEE-lee-ahs) (noun)
Literally, "father of the family." More generally, a figure of authority, both by blood and by custom.

My grandfather considered himself the PATER FAMILIAS and was never happier than when his children and grandchildren gathered around his chair to listen to him lay down the law about something.

pax (Latin) (paks) (noun)
Peace. We say it in Latin because there's some faint possibility of it being taken more seriously in that language than in English.
The two sides, after months of fighting, decided to declare PAX and go home—though without any measure of good feeling between them.

pax vobiscum (Latin) (PAKS wo-BIS-koom) (phrase)
Peace be with you. Although this is a salutation in the Catholic Mass, there's no reason why people from other religions—or no religions at all, for that matter—shouldn't say it to one another. They might even mean it.

per annum (Latin) (per AN-oom) (adv.)
Per year. Usually in reference to a sum of money to be paid or received once a year.
Tuition at our university is $75,000 PER ANNUM, but rest assured that your son or daughter will receive the finest education in return for this trifling sum. Of course, we can't make any guarantee that he or she will have a job afterward.

per ardua ad alta (Latin) (pare AHR-doo-ah ad AL-tah) (phrase)
Through difficulties to the heights. The motto of a number of universities, it is meant, no doubt, to remind students that the road to graduation is a challenging one and they will have to struggle to reach the dizzying goal of a bachelor's degree. The failure of most students to understand this concept can no doubt be attributed to the fact that they don't know enough Latin to understand what the sentence means.

per capita (Latin) (per KAP-i-ta) (adv.)
Literally, "for each head." For each person.
We've decided to allocate two slices of bread and three pieces of cheese PER CAPITA, which should help us survive until help arrives.

per diem (Latin) (per DEE-em) (adv./noun)
For each day. This sometimes refers to a sum of money allocated for expenses on a business trip.

My PER DIEM for trips is usually $75, but since I'm going to Vegas, I've asked them to raise it to $500. That should get me through the night.

P.

perestroika (Russian) (per-es-STROH-ee-kah) (noun)
Literally, "restructuring," this was a political movement within the Soviet Union in the 1980s that eventually led to the end of the U.S.S.R. (see **glasnost**). Initiated by Mikhail Gorbachev (1931–), it aimed at reducing the power of the Soviet bureaucracy and creating stronger ties between the Communist Party and the people. What it actually did was expose the corruption within all layers of the party and the Soviet government.

perpetuum mobile (Latin) (pare-PEH-too-oom MOH-bee-lay) (adv.)
A musical term that literally means "perpetual motion." In a piece of music, it indicates that a passage should be played at a rapid tempo. Alternately, it can indicate that a piece should be repeated indefinitely.

per se (Latin) (per SAY) (adv.)
As such.

My cousin isn't unemployed PER SE, but since he works for himself, and he's a lousy boss, he never asks very much of his employee, which means he tends to stay in bed until noon.

persona non grata (Latin) (per-SOHN-ah non GRAH-tah) (noun)
An unwelcome person. Someone not legally recognized.

Ever since that unfortunate incident involving the flight attendant, the poodle, and the Cheez Whiz, most airlines have declared me PERSONA NON GRATA.

pièce de résistance (French) (pee-ECE de ray-ZIS-tahns) (noun)
Literally, "A piece of resistance." Colloquially, the showpiece or centerpiece of something, usually a meal. The idea is that this is a dish that resists convention and makes the entire meal unique.

*Tonight for the PIÈCE DE RÉSISTANCE we have a casserole of
tripe and tuna, with a smidgeon of caviar to finish it off.*

pied-à-terre (French) (pee-EHD a TARE) (noun)
A temporary residence. A second home, usually a small apartment.
*Because I work in New York but live in Massachusetts, I have taken
a PIED-À-TERRE in Brooklyn so I have somewhere to stay during
the week.*

plotz (Yiddish) (PLOTZ) (verb)
To burst as a result of powerful emotional turmoil.
*So excited I am by this news that you and your fourth cousin Sylvia
are engaged, I'm going to PLOTZ. Sit down and we'll start plan-
ning the wedding.*

Plus ça change, plus c'est la même chose (French) (ploo sah
SHANZH ploo say lah MEM SHOWZ) (phrase)
The more things change, the more they remain the same. This comment has been attributed to Jean-Baptiste Karr (1808–1890), a
French critic and journalist who made the comment in 1849. He
perhaps had in mind the massive political uprisings across Europe
the previous year, which, although they resulted in changes in gov-
ernments, did not overthrow the established order.

> **Nota Bene**
> Although it's true that things often change only superficially,
> the 1848 uprisings in Europe did have one far-reaching effect.
> In Germany, two young men penned a document for the
> League of Just Men, in an attempt to establish its political pro-
> gram. The men were Karl Marx (1818–1883) and Friedrich
> Engels (1820–1895), and the pamphlet they produced was
> titled *The Communist Manifesto.*

poco a poco (Spanish) (POH-koh ah POH-koh) (adv.)
Little by little. A little bit at a time.
*Getting the piano up these twelve flights of stairs may seem like an
impossible job, but the three of us are accomplishing it POCO A
POCO.*

point d'appui (French) (PWAN dah-PWEE) (noun)
A point of appearance. In military usage, the point at which troops
are located before being flung into battle. A staging ground, as it
were.

> *We've placed our forces at a POINT D'APPUI behind this hill so
> they'll be invisible to the enemy. Of course, if the enemy has spy
> planes, we're screwed.*

Nota Bene

Among the most successful and largest staging operation in
history was that carried out by the Western Allies in 1944
on the eve of the invasion of France. Nearly 200,000 troops
were assembled in Britain, and on June 6 they crossed the
English Channel to land on the beaches of Normandy. The
German leadership had been convinced that the invasion,
when it came, would occur elsewhere (specially, at Cal-
ais) and thus the Allies gained a strategic foothold on the
Continent.

---

por favor (Spanish) (por fahv-OR) (interjection)
Please.

> *Could you get me another order of enchiladas and some cold beer to
> go with that, POR FAVOR? Gracias.*

posse comitatus (Latin) (POS-say kom-i-TAH-tus) (noun)
An act passed by Congress in 1878 that limits the degree to which
federal troops may be used to enforce the law. The act has been the
subject of a great deal of argument and was invoked in the 1960s
by Southern states, which claimed that under its provisions, the
federal government could not send in troops to states in the South
to enforce desegregation. President Eisenhower, however, invoked
legislation that allowed the federal government to send troops
when state authorities refused to suppress violence threatening
the lives and liberties of citizens. The result was that in 1958,
federal troops helped desegregate the high school in Little Rock,
Arkansas.

post hoc ergo propter hoc (Latin) (post hok ER-go PROP-ter hok) (phrase)

Literally, "After this, therefore that." A logical fallacy that states that because one action or event followed another, the first must necessarily have caused the second.

Nota Bene

During the television show *The West Wing*, President Josiah Bartlet had the following exchange with C.J., his press secretary; Josh, a staff member; and Leo, his chief of staff:

Bartlet: C.J., on your tombstone it's gonna read, "Post hoc ergo propter hoc."

C.J.: Okay, but none of my visitors are going to be able to understand my tombstone.

Bartlet: Twenty-seven lawyers in the room, anybody know, "Post hoc, ergo propter hoc"? Josh?

Josh: Ah, post, after hoc, ergo, therefore . . . After hoc, therefore something else hoc.

Bartlet: Thank you. Next? Leo.

Leo: "After it, therefore because of it."

Bartlet: "After it, therefore because of it." It means one thing follows the other, therefore it was caused by the other. But it's not always true. In fact it's hardly ever true. We did not lose Texas because of the hat joke. Do you know when we lost Texas?

C.J.: When you learned to speak Latin?

post scriptum (Latin) (post SKRIP-tum) (noun)
Usually abbreviated *P.S.*, this is an afterthought added at the end of a letter.

> *P.S. Can you stop by the store on the way home and pick up a gallon of rum, a gallon of rye, and a gallon of tequila? I feel like celebrating tonight.*

prêt-à-porter (French) (PRET ah por-TAY) (adj.)
Ready to wear; off the rack. Generally, clothes described this way are not as good as ones made to order.

> *I've got this party I'm going to tonight and all my good clothes are at the cleaner. I'm going to need to buy something PRÊT-À-PORTER. I just hope I don't look too tacky.*

prima facie (Latin) (PREE-mah FAH-kee-ay) (adv.)
Literally, "on first encounter." In legal terms, this refers to evidence that appears self-evident and needs no significant corroboration.

> *Your Honor, since my client is a quadraplegic, I wish to point out that the prosecution's argument that he is a smash-and-grab thief who snatches purses is PRIMA FACIE ridiculous.*

primum mobile (Latin) (PREE-mum MOH-bee-lay) (adj.)
First moved. In medieval astronomy, the outermost of the concentric spheres that held the planets and the stars and set them in their motion across the skies.

> **Nota Bene**
> Medieval astronomers believed that various heavenly bodies were affixed to crystalline spheres that moved in complicated patterns around Earth. This was, of course, in keeping with the church-inspired notion that Earth, God's creation, was at the center of the universe. At times, it was believed, the spheres vibrated against one another, causing noise and giving rise to the expression "music of the spheres."

primus inter pares (Latin) (PREE-mus in-ter PAH-rayz) (noun)
First among equals. In theory, the early Roman emperors, starting
with Augustus (63 B.C.– A.D. 14) were simply Senators who had
been temporarily elevated to command of the Roman state. Whether
Augustus believed this nonsense is open to question, but his succes-
sors certainly did not and accepted that they ruled as absolute mon-
archs. Today, more often than not the expression conceals a similar
fiction in various organizations.

*Some politicians maintain that the Speaker of the House is merely
PRIMUS INTER PARES, while others recognize him as a leader
who has been elevated to lead his party with absolute authority.*

prix fixe (French) (pree feeks) (noun)
In dining, a meal with a set price and set courses. Usually restaurants will offer both a *prix fixe* menu and one that includes *à la carte*
items.

*The PRIX FIXE dinner includes lobster and a chocolate mousse to
follow. I'm sold on that.*

pro bono publico (Latin) (pro BOH-noh PUB-li-koh) (adv.)
For the public good. In legal circles, cases are sometimes under-
taken by lawyers for greatly reduced fees (or, very occasionally, for
no fee) if they deem the case in question to be one that could have
a significant impact on the public welfare. Or, alternately, if it could
promote their careers.

pro forma (Latin) (pro FOR-mah) (adv.)
For form's sake. Just to conform to the rules.

*Before I offer you the position, could you just PRO FORMA fill out
an application. That'll make the folks in HR happy.*

pro rata (Latin) (pro RAH-tah) (adv.)
In proportion.

*I need you to bill the number of hours PRO RATA on this job, tak-
ing into consideration its benefit to the firm and how much time you
think it's going to take in the future.*

pure laine (French) (poor LEN) (adj.)

Literally, "pure wool," the term has come to mean true or loyal. Only the French, be it said, would be able to make the connection between sheep and politics, but then the French can connect pretty much anything to politics.

Before allowing him into our caucus at the convention, we've asked around to determine if he's PURE LAINE. It's all right. He's given lots of money to our wing of the party.

P

"Not only does the English language borrow words from other languages, it sometimes chases them down allyes, hits them over the head, and goes through their pockets."

—Eddy Peters

qua (Latin) (KWA) (adverb)
In the way of.

> *To discuss literature QUA literary theory, one must know the subject matter thoroughly.*

Quellenforschung (German) (kel-len-FOR-shung) (noun)
Study of the origins of a work of literature. German scholarship comes up with words like this; that is why German university professors, in all their photographs, tend to look ponderous and gloomy, as if they were thinking important thoughts of word significance rather than, I wonder how long this is going to take so I can get back to my beer and sausages.

> *If, for some reason, you should want a graduate degree in English, QUELLENFORSCHUNG is necessary.*

Quem di diligunt adulescens moritur (Latin) (kwem dee di-li-GUNT ad-you-LESS-kens MOR-ee-toor) (phrase)
Those whom the gods love, die young. Billy Joel (1949–) used this expression (in English) as the title of a song, "Only the Good Die Young," which, sadly, is probably the only way most people today know it.

> *The tragic death of the high school football player right after the big game illustrates that the Romans were right in saying QUEM DI DILIGUNT ADULESCENS MORITUR.*

Que sera sera (Spanish) (KAY ser-AH ser-AH) (phrase)
Whatever will be, will be. The title of a song made popular by Doris Day (1924–) from the Alfred Hitchcock film *The Man Who Knew Too Much*. The song became Day's signature tune and thus occupied big chunks of the airwaves during the late 1950s.

> *I think I may have failed my math exam, but in the overall scheme of things, QUE SERA SERA.*

Qui dormit non peccat (Latin) (kwee DOR-mit non pek-KAHT) (phrase)
He who sleeps does not sin. This may, perhaps, be the governing principle behind those students who sleep in class, since they

assume if they're not getting the answers right, at least, when in Slumberland, they're not getting them wrong.

Prior to robbing the bank at 4 o'clock in the morning, the gang should have remembered QUI DORMIT NON PECCAT.

quid pro quo (Latin) (KWID pro KWO) (phrase)

One thing is given in exchange for another. A standard clause of many contracts. It is also a possible basis for charges of sexual harassment, since in many circumstances there is an offer of job advancement in return for sexual favors.

Assuming that a QUID PRO QUO is sometimes required, Arthur gave his professor a bottle of whiskey in exchange for an A. Shortly afterward, a visit from the Dean reminded him that the university administrators did not look kindly upon bribery, at least when it wasn't extended to them.

Quidquid Latine dictum sit altum videtur (Latin) (KWID-kwid lah-TEE-nay DIK-tum sit AHL-tum wi-DAY-toor) (phrase)

Whatever is spoken in Latin seems wonderful. Literally, "Whatever spoken in Latin seems deep." This is a wise thing to remember, since unwelcome information can always be couched in impressive-sounding Latin phrases.

Attempting to impress his new in-laws, Mark peppered his speech with Latin phrases on the theory of QUIDQUID LATINE DICTUM SIT ALTUM VIDETUR.

Quis custodiet ipsos custodes (Latin) (kwis kus-TO-dee-et IP-sos kus-TOH-dayz) (phrase)

Who watches the watchers? This idea appears many times in popular culture: It is, for example, the title of an episode of *Star Trek: The Next Generation*, in which the native population of an M-class planet decides that Captain Picard of the starship Enterprise is a god.

In looking at today's government, how many times must we ask the question, QUIS CUSTODIET IPSOS CUSTODES. I mean, if we can't count on the people we elect, whom can we count on?

Q

quod erat demonstrandum (Latin) (KWAHD eh-RAHT dem-on-STRAHND-um) (phrase)
That which has been proven. Sometimes abbreviated QED, this is placed at the conclusion of a mathematical or logical proof to indicate that a point has been established.

All men are mortal. Socrates is a man. Therefore, QUOD ERAT DEMONSTRANDUM, Socrates is mortal.

Quo vadis (Latin) (kwo WAH-dis) (phrase)
Where are you going? According to the Acts of Peter, part of biblical apocrypha, Peter meets Jesus on the road while he (Peter) is fleeing execution in Rome. He asks, "Where are you going?" to which Jesus replies, "I am going to Rome to be crucified again." This confrontation stiffens Peter's backbone sufficiently that he continues his ministry and is eventually crucified (upside-down) in Rome— supposedly on the site of St. Peter's Basilica. The episode was the subject of a 1951 movie starring Robert Taylor and Deborah Kerr.

One of the first phrases I learned in Latin class was QUO VADIS. That's what the teacher asked me when I got up in the middle of class to go to the bathroom.

"Every American child should grow up knowing a second language, preferably English."

—Mignon McLaughlin, *The Neurotic's Notebook*

raconteur (French) (rah-kon-TUR) (noun)
A very talented storyteller; alternately, in some interpretations, one who loves to hear himself talk.
> *Everyone was enthralled by Alan's tale and said he was quite the* RACONTEUR.

raison d'être (French) (RAY-zohn de-tre) (phrase)
Literally, "reason for being." Colloquially, a justification for something or someone. The foundation of someone's existence.
> *Cooking was Julia Child's* RAISON D'ETRE.

rapprochement (French) (ra-prosh-MAHN) (noun)
Establishment of a harmonious relationship. Usually some sort of a truce between previously warring parties. Or, if one cares to be more cynical a là the great American humorist Ambrose Bierce: "Peace: A period of cheating between two periods of fighting."
> *At the end of the Civil War, Lee and Grant reached a* RAP-PROCHEMENT *after Grant allowed Lee's soldiers to keep their horses in order to help with the spring planting.*

rara avis (Latin) (RAH-rah AH-wis) (phrase)
Something rare. Literally, "rare bird."
> *A fountain pen these days is considered by some to be a* RARA AVIS.

> **Nota Bene**
> In the noir classic *The Maltese Falcon* by Dashiell Hammett (1894–1961), the rara avis at the heart of the story is, literally, a rare bird. Both the villains and the detective are searching for a fabulous treasure, a jewel-encrusted statue of a falcon, lost for centuries before surfacing in twentieth-century San Francisco.

Raus! (German) (ROWS) (interjection)
Out! Generally meaning, "Get out!"
> *The commandant blew a whistle and shouted "*RAUS!*" to get the POWs out of the barracks.*

Realpolitik (German) (REEL-pol-i-tik) (noun)
A system of diplomacy based on practical applications rather than theories. Literally, "real politics." It was particularly associated with the German chancellor Otto von Bismarck (1815–1898), through whose efforts the diverse states of north-central Europe were wielded into the German kingdom.

The German government believes itself to be based on REALPOLI-TIK rather than some high-flown, idealized notion of what government should be.

> **Nota Bene**
> Although Bismarck was the originator of Realpolitik, it has been practiced with avidity by many in the twentieth and twenty-first centuries. Outstanding in this regard has been Henry Kissinger (1923–), national security advisor and secretary of state in the Nixon administration. It was Kissinger who remarked, only partly in fun, "The illegal we do immediately; the unconstitutional takes a little longer."

réchauffé (French) (RAY-show-FAY) (noun)
Reheated leftover food. More generally, it can also a rehashing of stale ideas, exemplifying the French ability to meld philosophical discourse (or pretty much anything) with cooking.

After Thanksgiving, dinners for the next week tend to be RÉCHAUFFÉ. And at the end of that week, everyone is completely sick of turkey for another year.

recherché (French) (RAY-share-SHAY) (adjective)
Rare. More often, pretentious.

Mark's knowledge of wine is just too RECHERCHÉ for anyone to feel comfortable around him. He acts as if I'm an idiot for not tasting the difference between a chardonnay and a chablis.

reductio ad absurdum (Latin) (re-DUK-tee-oh ad ab-ZIR-dum) (phrase)
Reduce to the absurd. This is a logical fallacy often appearing in politics, in which one side tries to take the other side's arguments to what they view as their logical conclusion.

If we consider the Republican argument that lowering tax rates always increases government revenues, the REDUCTIO AD ABSURDAM would suggest that lowering the tax rate to 0 percent would lead to revenues growing an infinite amount.

Rem acu tetigisti (Latin) (rem AK-oo te-tee-GIS-tee) (phrase)
You have touched the matter with the needle. More familiarly, you have hit the nail on the head.
With your suggestion that since Rachel is a sociopath, perhaps we should reconsider making her the office manager, REM ACU TETIGISTI.

Nota Bene

Author P. G. Wodehouse (1881–1975) tended, in his stories of Bertie Wooster and Jeeves, to toss in various foreign terms and phrases. At one point, in the classic *Jeeves in the Morning,* Bertie makes a comment to which Jeeves replies, "Precisely, sir. Rem acu tetigisti."

"Rem—?"

"Acu tetigisti, sir. A Latin expression. Literally, it means 'You have touched the matter with a needle,' but a more idiomatic rendering would be—"

"Put my finger on the nub?"

"Exactly, sir."

Bertie is constantly astounded by his valet's erudition. "It beats me how you think of these things," he says.

Requiescat in pace (Latin) (RAY-kwis-kaht in PAH-kay) (phrase)
Rest in peace. A common inscription on gravestones.
For all of those who have been killed in senseless fighting, REQUIESCAT IN PACE.

Res ipsa loquitur (Latin) (rayz IP-sah LOW-kwit-er) (phrase)
The thing speaks for itself. The phrase is used as a legal term referring to a matter in which injury occurred due to circumstances that were inherently risky. Like most legal terms, it is designed to shelter the law from the understanding of ordinary people, who can thus continue to pay lawyers enormous sums to interpret it for them.

R

The Ford Company was liable for injuries caused by exploding Pintos under the doctrine of RES IPSA LOQUITUR. Presumably the car's manufacturers should have known the gas tanks would explode on rear-impact collisions.

retroussé (French) (REH-trew-say) (adjective)
Upturned, generally referring to a nose. A delightful feature on a woman's face; when it occurs on a man's face, he looks like Bob Hope.

Marion's nose has a RETROUSSÉ quality about it.

rigor mortis (Latin) (RI-gor MOR-tis) (noun)
The stiffness of death caused by muscular contraction. In humans it begins about three to four hours after death and lasts between forty-eight and sixty hours.

The body found in the alley was obviously dead, since RIGOR MORTIS had set in. From the degree of stiffness in the stiff, the CSI team was able to deduce the time of death.

roman à clef (French) (roh-MAHN ah KLAY) (phrase)
A novel featuring real people or events thinly disguised as fiction. Literally, "a novel with a key."

A good example of ROMAN À CLEF is Robert Penn Warren's All the King's Men, *which offers a version of the life of Louisiana politician Huey P. Long.*

"Whenever the literary German dives into a sentence, that is the last you are going to see of him till he emerges at the other side of his Atlantic with his verb in his mouth."

—Mark Twain

samizdat (Russian) (SAH-miz-daht) (noun)
A secret organization publishing banned literature. The word was also used in the Soviet Union to refer to banned literature itself, which was typed or hand-copied and secretly passed among dissidents.

> *In some countries, if you are going to print something denouncing the government, you have to organize a SAMIZDAT. In other countries, you just have to get on the Internet.*

Nota Bene

Prior to the collapse of the Soviet Union in 1989, the country had a long, rich samizdat tradition, extending back to the height of the Stalinist terror of the 1930s. Alexandr Solzhenitsyn (1918–2008) is the best known of the Russian dissidents who published some of his works in this manner; another included Roy Medvedev (1925–), author of the monumental history of the Stalinist era, *Let History Judge*. Roy's brother Zhores (1925–) authored a critique of the Stalinist "biologist" Trofim Lysenko (1898–1976) that was circulated surreptitiously in the U.S.S.R.

sanctum sanctorum (Latin) (SANK-tum SANK-tor-um) (noun)
Holy of holies. The word is often used to refer to the innermost part of a temple or other religious shrine, but it can have a broader meaning of a strictly private place of refuge.

> *Superman's Fortress of Solitude was his SANCTUM SANCTORUM. There he presumably sat around on furniture made from ice and brooded over whether to date Lois Lane or Lana Lang.*

sang-froid (French) (san FRWAH) (noun)
Extreme composure. Literally, "cold blood."

> *Laura showed considerable SANG-FROID when confronted by a huge, vicious dog on her afternoon walk. Rather than let it intimidate her, she emptied her water bottle over its head, whereupon the dog yelped and ran back into its yard.*

sans-souci (French) (SAHN soo-see) (adverb)
Carefree. Without worries.
> *Susie lived her entire life with a SANS-SOUCI attitude, ignoring creditors, spurned boyfriends, or anyone else that threatened to disturb her tranquility.*

> **Nota Bene**
> Frederick the Great (1712–1786), ruler of Prussia, didn't do things by halves. In the 1740s, he built a magnificent summer palace in Potsdam near Berlin and named it Sanssouci. Although small by the standards of the time, it was roomy enough that Frederick didn't have to worry about bumping into anyone. The goal of the architect seems to have been to design a building that minimized such problems as damp and heating, making it a palace literally "without cares."

Sauve qui peut! (French) (sohv kee PU) (phrase)
Save yourself. Generally this is in reference to a state of panic. Literally, "save who you can."
> *French passengers aboard the* Titanic *were screaming SAUVE QUI PEUT as the ship went down.*

savoir-faire (French) (SAH-vwahr FAIR) (noun)
Instinctive expertise. Literally, "to know to do." As well, it can imply the ability to say or do just the right thing.
> *Maria had great SAVOIR-FAIRE with computers and carried it off with such conviction that everyone was instantly convinced of her expertise.*

Schadenfreude (German) (SHAH-den-froid-eh) (noun)
Getting kicks out of the misery of others. Literally, "damage joy." A delightfully German word—who else but the Germans would have thought up something like this? The implication of the expression is that some measure of poetic justice is being served.
> *The arsonist experienced SCHADENFREUDE while watching the house burn, its inhabitants huddling miserably watching. It was fitting, since they had previously destroyed his home.*

schlemiel (Yiddish) (shle-MEEL) (noun)
A perpetually clumsy person. A bungler and a dolt.

Alison is a real SCHLEMIEL, because she broke the same ankle four times. And in the same place, too.

schlep (Yiddish and German) (shlep) (verb)
Carry or drag. The usual implication is that the object is unreasonably burdensome.

I had to SCHLEP a ten-pound art history textbook all over campus. Now my back is killing me.

schmaltz (Yiddish) (SHMALTZ) (noun)
Melted chicken fat; also overly sentimental

If you want to make matzo ball soup properly, use SCHMALTZ as well as matzo. Afterward, you can sit in the living room and watch a chick flick that's full of SCHMALTZ.

> **Nota Bene**
> Yiddish is not, as some people think, the language of all Jews. Instead, it is a fusion of High German with various dialects and languages, as well as Hebrew. It began in central Europe in the Ashkenazi culture and spread outward. In New York during the late nineteenth century and early twentieth century it was the lingua franca of Jewish immigrants from eastern Europe who crowded the slums of Lower Manhattan.

schmeer (also schmear, shmeer, and shmear) (Yiddish) (SHMEER) (noun)
A spread, usually for bagels.

An onion bagel is really good with a cream cheese and chive SCHMEER.

> **Nota Bene**
> Bagels, despite many conflicting stories about their ori-
> gins, are originally Polish, invented in the early seven-
> teenth century. The true bagel is a ring of dough, first
> boiled in water and then baked to give it a hard crust and
> a chewy interior. Real bagels are often topped with poppy
> seeds and flavored with onions or garlic. Fake bagels (nota-
> bly most of those made in pretentious little boutiques on
> the West Coast) are flavored with such abominations as
> sun-dried tomatoes and pulverized artichoke hearts. As
> any East Coast native will attest, the best bagels are found
> in New York. No contest.

schmo (Unknown) (shmoh) (noun)
A jerk. A variant of **schmuck**.
   Most of us try to avoid Dennis, since he's a real SCHMO.

schmuck (Yiddish) (shmuk) (noun)
Derogatory term for an individual. Literally, "penis." The come-
dian Lenny Bruce (1925–1966) claimed that he was arrested
for saying it on stage after an undercover Jewish police officer
determined that the meaning of the Yiddish term was obscene.
(A comment on the state of entertainment in the 1960s, as
opposed to now, when calling someone a schmuck on stage
would be considered hopelessly old-fashioned and polite.)
   Don't be such a SCHMUCK about sharing your cupcakes.

Schweinhund (German) (SHVINE-hoont) (noun)
Extremely offensive term for an individual. Literally, a "pig dog."
The English translation ("pig dog") pops up in a completely unlikely
context in the mouths of French soldiers in Monty Python and the
Holy Grail.
   *You stole my seat at the cafeteria, you SCHWEINHUND! I hope
   you're flatulent for the rest of the day.*

scire quod sciendum (Latin) (SKEE-rah kwod skee-EN-doom) (phrase)
To know what is worth knowing. Of course, one's evaluation of what precisely that is depends. An engineer would claim that anything that doesn't involve zeroes and ones is beneath his interest. We, on the other hand, coming from the humanities, believe that the full range of human artistic expression is a worthy subject of study—with the possible exception of the music of John Mayer.

> *Most professors claim a SCIRE QUOD SCIENDUM in their respective fields.*

Sedit qui timuit ne non succederet (Latin) (SAY-deet kwee TI-moo-it nay non su-KAY-der-et) (phrase)
"He who feared he would not succeed sat still." A quotation from the Roman poet Horace (65 B.C.–8 B.C.). Broadly, if you do nothing, you'll achieve nothing. This should be writ large on the diploma of every graduating senior.

semper fidelis (Latin) (SEM-per fee-DAY-lis) (adv.)
Always faithful.

> *The motto of the United States Marine Corps is SEMPER FIDELIS, often abbreviated as Semper Fi.*

shiksa (Yiddish and Polish) (SHIK-sah) (noun)
A Gentile, or non-Jewish, woman

> *Morrie's mother became very upset when she discovered he was dating a SHIKSA.*

shtick (Yiddish) (shtik) (noun)
A theme or a gimmick, often referring to comedy routines.

> *The comedy act of Stiller and Meara was known for the Irish girl marries Jewish guy SHTICK. Their son, Ben Stiller, is known for making a lot of bad movies (and a few good ones).*

> **Nota Bene**
> One of the great gatherings of Jewish comedians was the Comedians Round Table at the Hillcrest Country Club in Beverly Hills, California. Although not everyone there was Jewish, the majority were. Regular attendees included the four Marx Brothers (Groucho, Harpo, Chico, and Zeppo), Al Jolson, Eddie Cantor, Lou Holtz, and George Jessel. According to Harpo Marx (1888–1964), it was one of the funniest places in the world, but most of what was said wasn't printable.

sic (Latin) (seek) (adverb)
Literally, "thus." Used generally within quotations to indicate that an error within the quoted words appeared that way in the original version.
> *Marge wrote, "I think the Red Sox didn't live up to they're[SIC] potential this year."*

Sic transit gloria mundi (Latin) (sik TRAN-zit GLOH-ree-ah MOON-dee) (phrase)
Thus the glory of the world passes. Nothing lasts forever. The phrase is apparently an adaptation of words by Thomas à Kempis (1380–1471) in his book, *The Imitation of Christ*. It implies the end of something wonderful
> *Looking out over the ruins of the Waterloo battlefield, and thinking back on the glory that was the French Empire, Napoleon is said to have observed, "SIC TRANSIT GLORIA MUNDI."*

Sic vita est (Latin) (sik WEE-tah est) (phrase)
Such is life. An appropriate world view to take when it's Friday evening, you've got no place to go, and your entire paycheck has been eaten up by the rent that's due next week.
> *In times of stress, one should keep in mind SIC VITA EST and struggle on.*

sine qua non (Latin) (SEE-nay kwa NON) (phrase)
Something that is absolutely necessary. Literally, "that without which."

Talent is SINE QUA NON for success in show business. Well, on the other hand, there are the Kardashians, so I suppose anything's possible these days.

soi-disant (French) (SWAH deez-OHN) (adjective)
Self-named. The phrase normally carries a note of disbelief and derision.
The SOI-DISANT lawyer defending the murderer turned out to have failed the bar exam.

soignée (French) (SWAHN-yay) (adjective)
Elegant. Feminine form of *soigné,* carrying with it the connotation of something beyond the ordinary.
Jacqueline Kennedy was considered to be very SOIGNÉE. Some other first ladies, however, look as if they'd been dragged through a hedge backward, and Mary Todd Lincoln shows that some women just shouldn't ever wear purple.

soirée (French) (SWAH-ray) (noun)
A party, generally held in the evening, since the root word is *soir* (evening). This is the sort of affair that may provide a perfect opportunity to use some of the words and phrases contained in this book.
Marcus's New Year's SOIRÉE was the social event of the year.

sola gratia (Latin) (SOH-lah GRAH-tee-ah) (phrase)
By grace alone. A central doctrine associated with the Reformation of the sixteenth century.
The Reformers believed that you could get to heaven SOLA GRATIA.

Nota Bene
The Protestant Reformation covers a variety of events and activities that, during the sixteenth century, split the Catholic Church and eventually delivered much of Northern Europe to the forces of Protestantism. Insofar as it has a starting point, it's generally considered to be October 31, 1517, when Martin Luther (1483–1546) wrote to his bishop protesting the sale of indulgences by a member of the church. (Popular legend says that Luther nailed 95 theses to the church door in Wittenberg, Germany, but this may well have no basis in fact.)

Solvitur ambulando (Latin) (SAHL-wi-tur ahm-bu-LAHN-doh) (phrase)
Literally, "It is solved by walking." More generally, a dilemma can be solved through practice and experimentation.

I'm not sure whether, at this distance, I can hit that old lady with a coconut, but SOLVITUR AMBULANDO. I'll just have to try and see what happens.

sotto voce (Italian) (SOH-toh VO-chee) (adv.)
In a soft voice. Quietly.

Bedtime stories are often read SOTTO VOCE so as not to disturb the child once she falls asleep. Of course, the minute you get up to leave the room, she wakes up again.

soupçon (French) (SOOP-son) (noun)
A tiny bit. A morsel.

Arthur liked to add a SOUPÇON of truffle oil to his mashed potatoes to give them that special taste that only true gourmands can appreciate.

Sturm und Drang (German) (SHTURM und DRAHNG) (phrase)
Storm and stress. The name given to a school of German literature in the late eighteenth century, focusing on individual subjectivity and extreme emotional expression. For this reason, it is usually seen as a precursor of the Romantic movement in the nineteenth century. The most prominent figures associated with it were Johann Wolfgang von Goethe (1749–1832) in works such as *The Sorrows of Young Werther* and Friedrich von Schiller (1759–1805). Both men later broke from the movement.

The younger generation of Romantic poets were known for STURM UND DRANG in both their lives and their work.

sui generis (Latin) (SOO-wee GEN-air-is) (adjective)
In a class by itself. Unique.

Vincent van Gogh's paintings were SUI GENERIS, even compared with those of his post impressionist contemporaries.

summa cum laude (Latin) (SOO-mah koom LOW-day) (phrase)
With highest honors. The best possible way to graduate from college (see **cum laude** and **magna cum laude**).

Alicia graduated SUMMA CUM LAUDE from Princeton. Today she's waiting tables while hoping something opens up for a theater history major.

Nota Bene

Universities first arose during the twelfth century in western Europe. Among the earliest were the University of Paris and the University of Bologna. The following century saw the founding of the Universities of Oxford and Cambridge in England and in the fifteenth century, the University of St. Andrews. Students studied the *trivium* (grammar, rhetoric, and logic) and the *quadrivium* (arithmetic, geometry, music, and astronomy). Gradually, various schools within the universities became established, leading to more or less the structure we have today.

stet (Latin) (stet) (verb)
Literally, "Let it stand." Used in editing, this indicates that a change marked by the editor should not be made, leaving a word or phrase in the text which had been marked for elimination.
After a fierce bout of editing, James had to go through again and mark STET over half of his changes.

sub judice (Latin) (sub YOU-dik-ay) (adv.)
Before the court, but not yet settled. Under consideration. Generally speaking, attorneys and others connected with cases that are *sub judice* aren't supposed to comment in public on them . . . not that this stops anyone from doing so.
For most of the summer of 1994, the O. J. Simpson case was SUB JUDICE.

sub rosa (Latin) (sub ROH-zah) (adverb)
Secretly, surreptitiously. Literally, "under the rose."
The meetings of the College of Cardinals, when selecting a new pope, are held SUB ROSA in the Sistine Chapel in the Vatican to prevent any of its decisions from leaking out prematurely.

Nota Bene

The rose is a complex symbol whose significance dates back to ancient Egypt, where it was believed to be a sign of the god Horus. In the Middle Ages it became symbolic of the mysteries of heaven. Dante Alighieri (1265–1321) in his poem *The Divine Comedy* made Paradise in the shape of a rose, with the traveler penetrating ever deeper within the petals to discover God at the center. More recently, of course, the novelist and semiotician Umberto Eco (1932–) put the symbol at the heart of his bestselling medieval murder mystery and philosophical thriller *The Name of the Rose*.

S

"Language is the armory of the human mind, and at once contains the trophies of its past and the weapons of its future conquests."

—Samuel Taylor Coleridge

tabula rasa (Latin) (TAHB-you-lah RAH-sah) (noun)
Blank slate, literally "erased slate." This refers to the idea that people are born without innate knowledge and that whatever they know comes from experience and perception. Others argue that humans are born with an inherent set of precepts.

Many people believe that the mind of a baby is a TABULA RASA. I tend to wonder if babies are born with Annoying Genes.

Tempus fugit (Latin) (TEMP-us FOO-git) (phrase)
Time flies. The expression was first used by Virgil (70 B.C.–19 B.C.) in his poem *Georgics*. It is frequently inscribed on the dials of old clocks.

At the end of every school term, students understand the notion of TEMPUS FUGIT. Sadly, for many schoolchildren at the end of the day, time not only doesn't fly, it crawls.

terra firma (Latin) (TARE-rah FIR-mah) (noun)
Solid land. As opposed to water or air or, presumably, swamp land, quicksand, or an earthquake zone.

After landing from a turbulence-filled flight, Jason was glad to be on TERRA FIRMA.

terra incognita (Latin) (TARE-rah in-kog-NEE-tah) (noun)
Unknown land. The term, first used by Ptolemy (90–168) in his *Geography*, was placed on old maps to indicate lands that had not yet been explored. In modern usage, it can also refer to an as-yet-undeveloped body of knowledge.

To the early explorers, the New World was TERRA INCOGNITA.

tête-à-tête (French) (TAYT-ah-TAYT) (phrase)
An intimate conversation. Literally, "head to head." The sort of conversations that French people are accustomed to have in cafés while puffing on Galoises and sipping endless glasses of wine before slipping off discreetly for an **affaire de coeur.**

Marcia and John were having a romantic TÊTE-À-TÊTE that evening, one that was, unfortunately, interrupted by her husband.

Timeo Danaos et dona ferentes (Latin) (TIM-ay-oh DAHN-ay-os et DOH-nah fer-EN-tayz) (phrase)
I fear Greeks even bearing gifts. This quotation from *The Aeneid* by Virgil (70 B.C.–19 B.C.) refers to an episode at the end of the Trojan War. The Greeks who had besieged the city of Troy had, apparently, departed, leaving behind a great wooden horse. The Trojans prepared to bring the horse into the city as a symbol of their victory over the Greeks. However, the priest Laocoön sensed a trick and told the assembled Trojans, "I fear Greeks, even bearing gifts." He was overruled (and devoured by a serpent that came from the sea). As it turned out, of course, he was perfectly correct. That night, as the Trojans slept, Greek soldiers emerged from within the wooden horse and opened the city's gates to their compatriots, who had sailed back under cover of night. The sack of Troy and the slaughter of its inhabitants began with the treachery of the wooden horse.

> *Laocoön was right to say, TIMEO DANAOS ET DONA FEREN-TES, although in the end it did no good.*

Nota Bene
The story of the Trojan War and the fall of Troy is the most important myth of the ancient world. Contrary to popular impression, the poet Homer did *not* tell that story in *The Iliad*; rather he recounted an episode in the seventh year of the war in which the Greek champion Achilles (who probably looked nothing like Brad Pitt) killed the Trojan champion Hector. The most complete recounting of the end of the war and the episode of the Trojan horse is in Book ii of Virgil's *The Aeneid*, written at least 800 years after Homer.

Timor mortis conturbat me (Latin) (TIM-or MOR-tis kon-TUR-baht MAY) (phrase)
Fear of death bothers me. The phrase pops up in medieval English and Scottish poetry, doubtless reflecting the fact that the English and the Scots spent much of the Middle Ages waling on each other. Under such circumstances, it's hardly surprising that people would be disturbed by death.

For most people, the sentiment TIMOR MORTIS CONTURBAT ME is not unusual. Of course, there are a few others, and they become bungee jumpers.

touché (French) (too-SHAY) (interjection)
Literally, "touched." In a fencing match, when one combatant touches the other, he (or the referee) calls out this word to indicate a hit.
Georges cried, "TOUCHÉ!" as his sword struck Armand during their duel. Armand, bleeding from the blow, hardly needed Georges to tell him he was wounded.

tour de force (French) (tour de forss) (noun)
A show of skill. An exceptional achievement.
Emily's performance on her literature exam was a TOUR DE FORCE and earned her an A.

tout de suite (French) (toot SWEET) (phrase)
As soon as possible.
I need that report on my desk TOUT DE SUITE! If you can't manage that, you'd better start looking for another job.

tout le monde (French) (TOO leh mond) (phrase)
Everyone. Literally, "all the world."
I'm not ashamed of our love! I want to trumpet it to TOUT LE MONDE! But we'd better wait a little while before we tell your mother about it.

trompe l'oeil (French) (tromp LOY) (noun)
Optical illusion. Literally, "trick of the eye." This style was much used in the seventeenth century, particularly on ceiling paintings to give the illusion of expanded space. Its use dates back to ancient Rome, when fake doors and panels were sometimes painted on walls. The triumph of the art of perspective during the Renaissance meant that painters could more easily make use of this technique.
Most visual puzzles use a TROMPE L'OEIL effect.

"Language is the archives of history."

—Ralph Waldo Emerson

Übermensch (German) (EOO-ber-MENSH) (noun)
Literally, "overman." Superman; super-human being. This concept is particularly associated with the philosophy of Friedrich Nietzsche (1844–1900), who suggested that humans should reject philosophies that were built on mercy and charity (he particularly had Christianity in mind) and strive toward the creation of a human who rose above lesser races and showed the way toward a brighter future.

Hitler was looking for the ultimate ÜBERMENSCH in his myth of the blond Aryan race; curiously he himself was short and dark.

> **Nota Bene**
> Nietzsche's philosophy has had a long, controversial life. He is often seen as a philosophic predecessor to Nazism and totalitarianism in general. He was also at the heart of one of the most notorious murder cases in the twentieth century, long after he himself was dead. In the 1924 Leopold and Loeb case in Chicago, two wealthy young men who had immersed themselves in Nietzsche's thought murdered a young boy to prove their intellectual superiority over the police. They were quickly caught and only escaped the death penalty because of the pleading of the famous defense attorney Clarence Darrow (1857–1938).

Ubi solitudinem faciunt pacem appellant (Latin) (OO-bee sol-i-TOOD-in-em FAHK-ee-unt PAH-kem ah-PELL-aHnt) (phrase)
They make a desert and call it peace. A bitter observation by the Roman historian Tacitus (56–117) that might, with justice, be applied to any number of today's battlefields, starting with Baghdad.

ultra vires (Latin) (UL-tra WEE-rayz) (adv./adj.)
Beyond power; generally, legal. If a company enters a contract concerning something over which it has no authority, the contract may be ruled *ultra vires*.

> *Richard Nixon felt himself to be ULTRA VIRES, but the Senate Watergate Committee and the House Judiciary Committee soon disabused him of that notion.*

ultima ratio (Latin) (UL-tima RAHT-eo) (noun)
The last argument.
   Making a last ditch effort to win the debate, Alan presented what he considered to be his ULTIMA RATIO.

Ursprache (German) (oor-SHPRAK-eh) (noun)
An original language. The foundation language of other languages.
   Indo-European is the URSPRACHE language of most Western languages.

> **Nota Bene**
> In 1786, the English scholar Sir William Jones (1746–1794) delivered a paper to the Asiatic Society in which he suggested that Sanskrit had so much affinity with both Latin and Greek "that no philologer could examine them all three without believing them to have sprung from some common source, which, perhaps, no longer exists." This was the beginning of the study of Indo-European, a linguistic group that links a vast number of languages including English, German, French, Latin, Greek, Sanskrit, Farsi, and others.

ut infra (Latin) (ut IN-frah) (phrase)
In bibliographic notation and scholarly discourse, as follows.
   The idea discussed UT INFRA needs more consideration.

ut supra (Latin) (ut SOO-prah) (phrase)
As previous. The opposite of *ut infra*.
   Please refer to the figures UT SUPRA to make your decision.

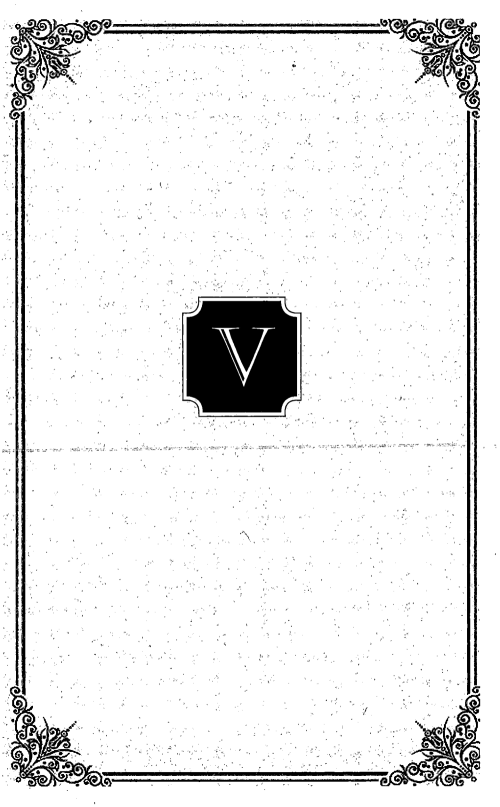

vade mecum (Latin) (WAH-day MAY-kum) (noun)
Something carried about. Literally, "that which goes with me." Generally a handbook or reference book that can be carried everywhere and consulted.
> *For my cousin, her atlas is her VADE MECUM, since she fears getting lost. No, really. Even going to the grocery store and back.*

vae victis (Latin) (why WEEK-tees) (phrase)
Sorrow to the defeated; woe to the conquered. According to the Roman historian Livy (59 B.C.– A.D. 17), an ancient foe of Rome conquered the city, and the Romans complained about the conditions he imposed on them. To which the conquerer quite reasonably replied, in effect, "I won! Deal with it!"
> *If you don't like having to pay off your bet, VAE VICTIS! You shouldn't have wagered against me in the first place.*

Veni, vidi, vici (Latin) (WAY-nee WEE-dee WEE-kee) (phrase)
"I came, I saw, I conquered." The words attributed to Julius Caesar (100 B.C.–44 B.C.) after his conquest of a city in Turkey.

Verba volant, scripta manent (Latin) (WARE-bah WHO-lahnt, SKRIP-tah MAH-nent) (phrase)
Spoken words leave, written words stay. A comment on the superfluousness of speech as opposed to writing. Today, of course, "writing" means texting and tweeting, something that seems far more insubstantial than many spoken words. The source of the original Latin proverb is unknown.
> *Since we know of little or nothing that Shakespeare's contemporaries said, we can observe of the Bard's writings, truly, VERBA VOLANT, SCRIPTA MANENT.*

verbatim (Latin) (wehr-BAY-tem) (adv.)
Exact words. Literally. Word for word.
> *In high school, my father had to know the "Rime of the Ancient Mariner" VERBATIM. Not only that, he had to recite it in front of a school assembly. His eye still twitches when he remembers the experience.*

verboten (German) (vare-BOHT-en) (adjective)
Forbidden.
Cheating on tests is strictly VERBOTEN.

verklempt (Yiddish) (vare-KLEMPT) (adjective)
Highly emotional.
I was VERKLEMPT at my daughter's wedding when I saw her coming down the aisle in white.

Veritas vincit (Latin) (WARE-ee-tas WIN-kit) (phrase)
Truth conquers. It would be nice to believe in this, but political campaigns have a way of convincing us otherwise. Still, it's nice to be optimistic, so if someone makes a particularly cynical comment to you, you can always toss this back at them.
As time goes by, it becomes clearer that in all things VERITAS VINCIT. Just because my lying sack of excrement of a husband is spreading rumors about me now doesn't mean they'll last forever.

via dolorosa (Latin) (WEE-ah dol-or-OH-sa) (noun)
The sorrowful way. Refers to Jesus's journey to his crucifixion. Since the eighteenth century, Christians have claimed to know the route within the Old City of Jerusalem that Jesus walked. Today it is the site of much pilgrimage and includes nine Stations of the Cross. More generally, the term can be applied to any path filled with tribulation.
On his way to his calculus exam, Marcus felt as though he were walking the VIA DOLOROSA.

videlicet (Middle English by way of Latin) (WEE-day-LEE-kit) (adverb)
Namely.
The movie Highlander *establishes that there can be only one immortal, VIDELICET Duncan MacLeod.*

vis-à-vis (French) (VEEZ-ah-VEE) (preposition, noun, or adverb)
Literally, "face to face." More generally, compared to.
I would certainly rather take an English literature course than something required, VIS-À-VIS math.

Vita summa brevis spem nos vetat incohare longam (Latin) (WEE-tah SOO-mah BREH-wis spem nos WAY-taht in-co-HAH-ray LONG-ahm) (phrase)

The brief span of life gives us little hope of longevity. Yet another depressing observation from the poet Horace (65 B.C.–8 B.C.), who must have been a big laugh at Roman parties. Still, this sort of thing fits into the general Roman cultural ethos of the first century B.C., when poets were expected to declaim about the futility of human endeavor.

Vive la différence (French) (VEEV lah dee-fay-RAHNS) (phrase)

Hooray for differences! Literally, "long live the difference." Particularly applied to the two sexes, it implied pleasure in flirtation.

Benjamin Franklin's view of women was definitely one of VIVE LA DIFFÉRENCE!

> **Nota Bene**
>
> Benjamin Franklin (1706–1790) was, as is well known, a founding father of the United States and the wise elder statesman who kept negotiations over the Declaration of Independence from collapsing. He was also an incurable womanizer. By the age of twenty-four he had an illegitimate son, William, who later sided with the Tories during the American Revolution and was permanently estranged from his father.

volte-face (French) (volt FAHSS) (noun)

About face. Make a change of directions, often in a policy.

Nixon's trip to China signaled an abrupt VOLTE-FACE by the United States on its Chinese foreign policy. For years afterwards, people said, "Only Nixon could have gone to China."

vorlage (German) (fohr-LAHG-eh) (noun)

Literally, "forward leaning." Generally refers the position of a skier who leans forward without lifting the heels from the skis.

Jean-Claude Killy had excellent VORLAGE during his Olympic competition.

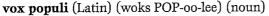

Voulez-vous coucher avec moi (French) (VOO-lay voo koo-SHAY ah-vek MWAH) (phrase)
Would you sleep with me? Literally, "Do you want to go to bed with me?" Keep in mind that this question, when posed at the end of a date, always sounds better in French than in English.

Labelle's hit "Lady Marmalade" contains the immortal question, "VOULEZ-VOUS COUCHER AVEC MOI?"

vox populi (Latin) (woks POP-oo-lee) (noun)
Voice of the people. Sometimes referring to media interviews conducted with the "man on the street." More generally, this refers to the idea of popular will.

Elections in this country are supposed to reflect the VOX POPULI, but—as we've seen in several recent elections—they very often don't.

Wanderjahr (German) (VAHN-dare-yar) (noun)
Wandering year. A year in which an apprentice wanders or takes off in order to improve her or his skills.

> *After graduating from college, Fred decided to take a WANDER-JAHR and travel around Europe in order to improve his language skills.*

Wanderlust (German) (VAHN-dare-lust) (noun)
Desire to wander. Found in the traditions of German Romanticism, which stressed the rootless, restless character of literary heroes, this concept pervades a great deal of nineteenth-century German literature. Only the Germans could have come up with a single word for it.

> *Tatania was unable to settle down anywhere for very long because of her intense WANDERLUST.*

Weltanschauung (German) (VELT-ahn-shahng) (noun)
A comprehensive, specific view of the world, often reflecting a fear or concern.

> *Aidan's WELTANSCHAUUNG made it difficult for him to meet new people.*

Weltgeist (German) (VELT-giyst) (noun)
World spirit. The motivating concept of the world. Something that is behind all the phenomena that we can perceive.

> *The Romantic poets believed that the WELTGEIST was Nature.*

Weltschmerz (German) (VELT-shmertz) (noun)
World weariness. A sense of disillusionment with society, usually leading the hero to wander off. (See **Wanderjahr**.)

> *One of the main characteristics of the Byronic Hero is a pervasive WELTSCHMERZ.*

Wunderbar (German) (VUN-dare-bahr) (adj.)
Wonderful! Excellent!

> *In German beer gardens, the patrons often shout WUNDERBAR!, particularly after hoisting a few steins.*

Wunderkind (German) (VUN-dare-kint) (noun)
Wonder child, usually refers to a prodigy. Someone who achieves success at an early age or stands out from her or his contemporaries.

In computer circles, Bill Gates can be considered a WUNDER-KIND, although the late Steve Jobs would probably have disputed that.

"That woman speaks eight languages and can't say no in any of them."

—Dorothy Parker

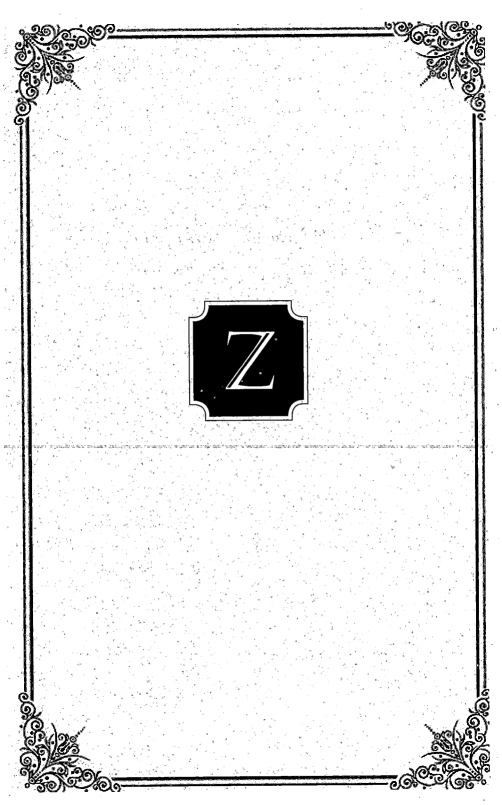

zaftig (Yiddish, from German) (ZAF-tig) (adjective)
Full figured; plump. In some respects, this word conveys the suggestion of sexiness.

> *Anna Nicole Smith was extremely ZAFTIG—more so at some times than others.*

Zeitgeist (German) (ZIYTE-giyst) (noun)
The general climate of any given era in time. Another one of those German words that have a precise philosophical meaning if you're German and are completely confusing and frustrating if you're not.

> *Phil Ochs's protest songs exemplified the ZEITGEIST of the Vietnam War era.*

About the Authors

Dr. Linda Archer received her MA in English from Bowling Green State University and her PhD in English literature from the University of Toledo. For more than twenty years, she has alternately inspired and terrified students by demanding that they read literature, talk about it, and even think about it intelligently. This has had, admittedly, mixed results, but on the whole she's satisfied that she's corrupted a few innocent minds along the way by making them read Byron's poetry.

She lives in Wareham, Massachusetts, with her husband and two cats, who, if they had an ounce of conscience between them, would get up off the floor and catch bugs or something.

Peter Archer received an MA from the University of Toledo and an MLitt from the University of St. Andrews. During a life that has seen its fair share of weird jobs (to give you an idea, he was at different times a pit clerk at the Chicago Mercantile Exchange and a political activist and production editor for a left-wing newspaper in New York City), he's acquired a reasonable vocabulary and a fund of anecdotes with which he bores the fur off the cats, since no one else will listen to them.

He lives in Wareham, Massachusetts, with his wife and the cats.

Index